Favourite Toys

JEAN GREENHOWE

Favourite Toys

Cuddly toys and dolls to make

HAMLYN

To Gaye

Acknowledgments

The toy designs in this book were originally featured in WOMAN'S WEEKLY magazine, and the author would like to express her thanks to the editor and all home department staff for their assistance and co-operation during the preparation of this book.

The author and publishers also wish to thank IPC Magazines, publishers of WOMAN'S WEEKLY, for their kind permission to reproduce their photographs.

Front cover: Jennifer Rag Doll (*see page 60*)
Back cover: Elephants (*see page 108*)
Endpapers: Dormouse House (*see page 84*)
Frontispiece: Wigwam (*see page 104*)
Below: Teaching Teddy (*see page 116*)

CONTENTS

First published in 1985 by
Hamlyn Publishing
a division of The Hamlyn Publishing Group Limited
Bridge House, London Road,
Twickenham, Middlesex

ISBN 0 600 50039 X

Printed in Italy

INTRODUCTION

This book is a follow-up to Cuddly Toys and Dolls *and it contains an even wider variety of things to make. There are instructions and patterns for over 50 toys, including rag dolls (to dress and undress), large and small furry animals, dolls' houses, play houses (for children to inhabit) and novelty toys.*
Some of the patterns are printed full-size for tracing directly off the pages. For the larger toys the patterns are printed on grids for easy scaling up to full size.
I have enjoyed designing and making the toys in this book for WOMAN'S WEEKLY *and am now delighted to see them all gathered together in one volume.*

TIPS FOR TOYMAKERS

(to be read before making any of the toys)

Instructions

First and foremost, do read the instructions! They contain all the information you need to make a toy just like the one shown in the illustration.

Safety first

Do make sure that the toy you are making is suitable for the person for whom it is intended. Very young children should not be given toys containing any dangerous items such as buttons or beads, which could become detached and swallowed. Felt eyes and noses are much safer than glass or plastic – however securely these may be fixed.

Equipment required

Dressmaking equipment: You need all the ordinary items as used for dressmaking – sewing machine, sewing threads, sharp scissors (large and small pairs), sewing needles, tape measure, etc.
Ruler: Marked with metric and imperial measurements.
Pins: Large glass- or plastic-headed pins are the best kind to use when making soft toys, as they are much easier to see and handle than ordinary pins. To avoid the danger of any pins being left in the toy accidentally, use a limited number and count them at each stage of making.
Tweezers: These can be very useful when handling small pieces of fabric or felt – for example, when glueing facial features in place. Tweezers can also be used to turn very small pieces right side out after stitching.
Compasses: A pair of inexpensive school compasses will be found invaluable for drawing out small circular patterns. Very large circles outside the span of your compasses can be drawn as described in the section headed *Copying the patterns.*
Old scissors: It is a good idea to keep an old pair of scissors just for cutting card and paper because these will blunt your good scissors.
Leather punch: Although this is not essential, a punch is extremely useful for cutting perfect tiny circles from felt, for small dolls' and animals' eyes. The felt should first

Left Football Mascot. Instructions begin on page 52

be treated with adhesive as described in the next paragraph.

Adhesive

Use an all-purpose clear adhesive such as UHU. This adhesive dries very quickly and also remains flexible after it is dry. Before cutting out felt facial features (or any other small felt pieces which are to be stuck in place on the toy), first spread the back of the felt with adhesive, then work it into the felt with the fingers and leave to dry. When felt is treated in this way the cut-out shapes will have smooth well-defined edges. This method should not of course be used for pieces of felt which are to be stuffed.

Unwanted smears of UHU can be removed by dabbing with a cloth dipped in acetone. Take care when using acetone as it is highly inflammable.

Measurements

The sizes given throughout the instructions in this book have been worked out individually both in metric and imperial, so that in many instances the conversions seem to be inconsistent and measurements do not always convert accurately from one to the other. This rounding-off of measurements is to avoid having awkward sizes, when a little extra either way will make no difference to the appearance of the finished toy.

On some of the diagrams, metric measurements only are given, for clarity. In these cases follow the metric sizes.

Copying the patterns

If full-size patterns are given for a toy, these can be traced directly off the pages on to thin strong paper, such as ordinary writing paper. First follow any special notes in the instructions regarding the patterns, then after tracing and cutting out the patterns, mark on all details and lettering.

Patterns for the larger toys are given scaled down on grids ruled to represent 1 cm, 2 cm or 5 cm squares, etc. For drawing out such patterns to full size, you can buy packets of dressmaker's metric graph paper from dress fabric shops or haberdashery departments. This paper is usually divided into 1 cm squares with a heavier line ruled at 5 cm intervals.

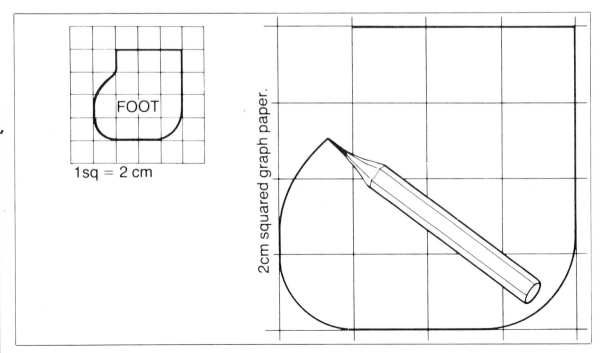

FOOT

1 sq = 2 cm

2cm squared graph paper.

Diagram 1 Drawing out full-size patterns on to graph paper from the scaled down diagram (shown above)

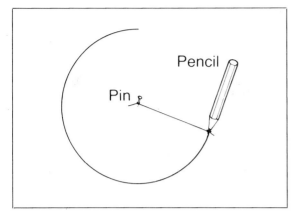

Diagram 2   How to draw large circles using pencil, a pin and a length of string

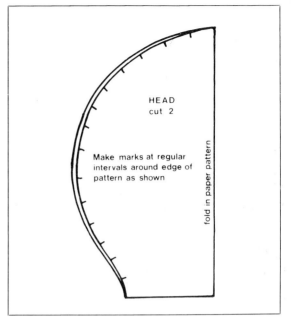

Diagram 3

If the scaled-down diagram states 'one square = 2 cm', then use a coloured pen or pencil to over-rule the graph paper every 2 cm. Now, following the scaled-down pattern outlines square by square, draw the same shapes on to the 2 cm graph paper as shown in diagram 1 (*opposite*). Follow the same procedure for any other sizes quoted on the diagrams.

For circular patterns the measurement given is usually the diameter (the distance across the centre) of the circle. When drawing circles set your compasses to the radius measurement, i.e. *half* the diameter. To draw circles which are larger than your compasses can make, take a length of thin string and knot one end around a pencil point. Now tie a knot in the string, the required radius measurement away from the pencil point, keeping the string taut as you measure. Now draw the circle as shown in diagram 2 (*above*).

When measurements for simple shapes are given in the instructions (such as squares, rectangles or triangles), you can draw these directly on to the wrong side of the fabric before cutting out. However, if the toy is to be made more than once, it is a good idea to cut paper patterns for such shapes and mark on all the details for future use.

Seams

Seams and turnings are allowed on the pattern pieces as stated in the instructions for each toy. Join fabric pieces with right sides facing unless otherwise stated.

To join the edges of large fabric or fur fabric pieces together accurately, proceed as follows. First of all, if the pattern is symmetrical, fold it in half as shown in diagram 3 (*above*). This shows the head pattern for the Best-dressed Doll on page 71. Now make pencil marks around the edge of one half of the pattern at intervals as shown on the diagram. Mark the other half of the pattern in the same way, matching the marked lines. If the pattern is not symmetrical, simply make marks at intervals all round the edge.

Now pin the pattern on to the fabric and cut out the shape. Before removing the pattern, lift it away from the fabric at each marked point and make a mark on the fabric at these positions. When pinning and stitching the fabric pieces together, match the marked points all round.

To mark dart lines, or other points on the paper pattern, on to the fabric, simply pierce the pattern along the dart lines at intervals with a sharp pencil point, pushing the point of the pencil into the fabric.

Fur fabric

There are various types of fur fabric available, with long or short pile and polished or unpolished surfaces. Short-pile fur fabric is

Above Punch and Judy Booth. Instructions begin on page 120

used for the toys in this book unless otherwise stated. If you have difficulty obtaining fur fabrics, see the list of suppliers at the end of the book.

On fur fabric, the fur pile lies smooth and flat if stroked in one direction, and will lift up if stroked in the opposite direction. On patterns for fur fabric toys, the direction of the 'smooth stroke' of the fur pile is indicated by an arrow on each pattern piece. Always take care to cut out the pieces so that the smooth stroke of the fur pile follows the direction of the arrows.

Fleecy fabric is also required for some of

the toys. This fabric, sold for making dressing gowns, etc., has a knitted backing and is brushed on the right side to form a soft furry surface. It does not have a pile with a smooth stroke like the other fur fabrics.

To cut out fur fabric pieces, pin the patterns, one at a time, to the wrong side of the fabric then snip through the back of the fabric only, so as not to cut through the fur pile on the right side. When cutting a pair of pieces, always take care to reverse the pattern before cutting the second piece.

To join fur fabric pieces, place the pieces right sides together, tucking in the fur pile at

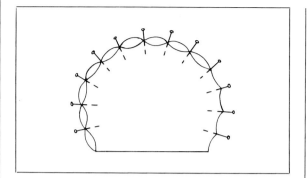

Diagram 4   Holding fur fabric pieces together with pins before sewing seams

the raw edges, then push in pins at right angles to the raw edges all round, as shown in diagram 4 (*above*). After sewing, remove all the pins, then turn right side out and pick out the fur pile trapped in the seam with the point of a pin.

Working with felt

Because felt is a non-woven fabric, it is often supposed that it has no grain. However, it

Diagram 5   Cutting out felt pieces

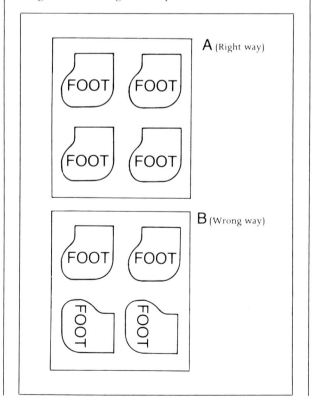

does have varying amounts of stretch when pulled lengthways and sideways, as well as stretch across the bias. When using felt for stuffed toys, always cut any identical pieces so that they lie in the same direction, parallel with the selvedge, or a straight edge if a square of felt is being used.

Diagram 5A (*below left*) shows an example of the correct way to cut the pieces for a doll's feet. If the feet are cut as shown in diagram 5B (*below left*), there may be differences in size after stuffing due to the felt stretching more in one direction than the other.

If the 'maximum stretch' of the felt is marked by arrows on the pattern pieces, be sure to cut out the pieces of felt accordingly.

Knitting yarn

When yarn is quoted in the materials for a doll or toy, this means knitting yarn, usually double knitting, unless other plys are mentioned. Some of the dolls in the book have yarn hair and it is also used occasionally for working facial features on other toys.

Making rag dolls

Using woven fabrics: Any fine, closely-woven calico, cotton or poly/cotton fabric is suitable for doll-making. While pink and peachy shades look best, cream or white can also be used. Pale pink is sometimes difficult to get in a dress fabric, but may be obtainable as sheeting. Many shops now have sheeting by the metre for making duvet covers, etc. If you do a lot of doll-making it is worth looking out for sale or bargain offers of sheets in the larger chain stores. A sheet bought in this way can work out cheaper than buying fabric by the metre.

Always cut out the doll pieces on the straight grain of the fabric unless the pattern indicates otherwise. Use a small machine stitch, and trim seams around all the curved parts to about 3 mm ($\frac{1}{8}$ in). After stuffing, any puckers in the seams can be ironed out as follows. Pinch the toy tightly between finger and thumb to force the stuffing against the puckered seam, then rub the seam against a warm iron.

Using stockinette: Cotton stockinette, in flesh or cream colour, is available by the metre specifically for making dolls. If you have difficulty obtaining stockinette, see the list of suppliers on page 139. Alternatively, discarded plain white stockinette vests or T-shirts can be used instead. These can be tinted pink if desired, following the dye-maker's instructions. When dyeing fabric remember that the colour always looks darker when the fabric is wet. Test a small cutting in the dye solution first.

Although stockinette will stretch in any direction when pulled, it usually stretches most across the width, as in hand-knitted fabric. The direction of 'most stretch' is indicated by arrows on each pattern piece or in the instructions when making dolls from stockinette.

Use a small machine stitch when sewing stockinette, stretching the seams slightly as you stitch, so that the threads will not snap when the pieces are stuffed. Trim the seams around all the curves to about 3 mm ($\frac{1}{8}$ in).

Dolls' hair

Cutting a number of equal lengths of knitting yarn for a doll's hair is a simple matter if you first wind the yarn into a hank. Select an object of suitable size to wind the yarn around – for example, a large book or the back of a chair. Note that the object should be somewhat longer than the required lengths, because the yarn will stretch slightly as it is wound.

After winding your hank, any kinks in the yarn can be removed as follows. Using two wooden spoons or any similar long-handled cooking utensils, slip the handles through each end of the hank. Stretch the hank tightly and steam it, by holding it over a pan of boiling water. Finally, cut through the hank at each end and trim the yarn strands to the length required.

Colouring cheeks

Use an orange-red pencil for colouring a doll's cheeks and always try the effect on an oddment of fabric first. For dolls made from woven fabric, gently rub the side of the pencil tip (not the point) over the cheek area. If the colour is too strong or uneven, some of it can be removed by rubbing gently with a soft eraser. For stockinette dolls which are very firmly stuffed, use the same method. For lightly stuffed stockinette dolls, moisten the pencil tip and apply a little colour at the centre of each cheek. Blend the colour over the cheek area with a bit of damp fabric.

Stuffing the toy

Many types of filling are available for toy-making. Foam chips should be avoided because they can be highly inflammable. Kapok is very good, but rather messy to work with as the fibres fly everywhere. Man-made fibre fillings are very clean to work with, and they have the added advantage of being washable. These fillings come in several grades, ranging from luxury high bulk white polyester to inexpensive multi-coloured filling, for use only when the colour will not show through the 'skin' of the toy.

For rag dolls and small to medium-sized soft toys, the most expensive polyester filling is really the best buy. Since it goes further (due to its high bulk quality) this filling can be just as economical to use as a cheaper type, where more filling would be required. For larger items, such as the sit-upon toys which need to be firmly stuffed, the cheaper fillings are very good.

Lumpy toys are usually the result of uneven stuffing, because small gaps are left where one piece of filling ends and the next begins. This happens most frequently in narrow pieces such as the limbs of a rag doll. When stuffing these, take a large handful of filling (polyester, not kapok which falls apart), and tease it into an elongated shape. Push one end of the filling into the end of the limb, then gradually feed in the filling with the fingers, trying to keep it in a continuous piece. Keep feeling the limb as it is stuffed, both inside and outside, taking care to fill any empty areas. When the piece of filling is almost finished, introduce one end of another piece in the same way, so that the fibres of the first piece will blend with the next.

If the limb is too narrow to get a finger inside, push in filling with the end of a pencil

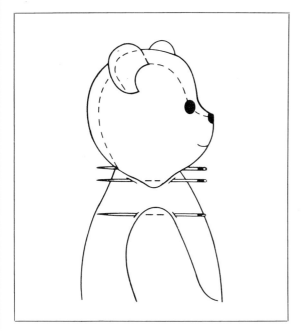

Diagram 6 Use darning needles to hold the head or limb to the body before sewing in place

or knob of a knitting needle. To stuff very small toys, use tweezers.

Attaching a head or limbs

To hold the head or limb of a toy securely to the body while sewing it in place, use darning needles instead of pins. Push the needles first into the body fabric, then into the head or limb, then back into the body fabric as shown in diagram 6 (*above*).

Ladder stitch

This stitch is used for closing the opening on a soft toy after stuffing. The raw edges of the

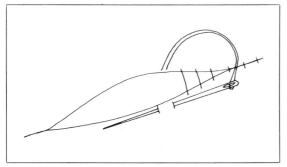

Diagram 7 Ladder stitch

fabric are turned in at the seam line, then the folded edges are laced together from side to side forming stitches which look like a ladder. Use strong double thread and take small, straight stitches alternately along one side then the other. After working a few stitches, pull the thread up tight, thus bringing the fabric edges together (*see diagram 7, below left*). Ladder stitch can also be used to make an invisible join when attaching the head or limb of a toy to the body.

Making a face

The age and character of a doll or toy are mainly determined by the positioning of the facial features. For a child-like appearance the eyes should be placed half-way down the face. If they are too close together the face will look mean, too far apart and the eyes will be frog-like. Therefore if measurements are given in the instructions for placing facial features, always follow these and your toy should look exactly like the one in the illustration.

If the eyes are made from felt, first pin them to the face, pushing the pins straight through the eyes and into the toy. Now check that they are level and centrally placed on the face by looking at the toy in a mirror. Any irregularities will show up immediately. The same method can be used if eyes and noses are to be embroidered, by pinning small paper shapes to the face before actually marking the fabric. An embroidered mouth line can be marked in the same way using a short length of thick thread or yarn pinned to the face as a guide.

When embroidering facial features, secure the knotted end of the thread in a place where it will not be seen on the finished toy – for example, at the back of a doll's head or under the position of a felt eye or nose on an animal. Use a long darning needle to take the thread through the toy to the position of the embroidered feature. Work the feature using a small sewing needle, then use the darning needle to take the thread back through the toy as before and fasten off the thread.

When sewing or glueing felt features on a fur fabric toy, snip away the fur pile beneath the felt before fixing it in place.

1
LARGE
SOFT TOYS

Cuddly Koalas

The koala twins measure about 40 cm (16 in) tall. You can make them from pale fawn fur fabric using white fur fabric for their chests and shaggy white fur fabric to line their ears. They each have three outfits of clothes — cosy sleeping suits (the same style for both bears), swimsuits, and playclothes (dungarees and sundress).

The Koalas

You will need: 60 cm ($\frac{3}{4}$ yd) of 138 cm (54 in) wide fawn fur fabric; 600 g (1 lb 5 oz) of stuffing; oddments of long- and short-pile white fur fabric for fronts of ears and chest pieces; scraps of black felt; metric graph paper; adhesive.

Notes: Copy the patterns on to graph paper, square by square; each square on diagram = 5 cm. See page 24.

Mark points A and B on body pieces and points C and D on arm pieces. Mark mouth line on wrong side of each front head piece and also mark centre of each eye with a length of coloured thread taken through to right side of fabric.

5 mm ($\frac{1}{4}$ in) seams are allowed on fur fabric pieces unless otherwise stated.

Body and head

Take the front head pieces and, on the wrong side of each one, machine stitch over the mouth line about six times using black thread, to make a thick line. Join them at centre front edges.

Join the body front pieces at centre front edges, from point A to neck edge, leaving a gap in the seam as shown on pattern. Gather neck edge of head front to fit neck edge of body front, then join neck edges matching centre front seams.

Join back head pieces at centre back edges. Join back body pieces at centre back from point B to neck edge. Now join neck edges of these pieces matching centre back seams.

Join entire front of koala to back, round sides of head and body, then round legs, matching points A and B. Turn right side out through front opening. Stuff head firmly, taking care to push stuffing in well at sides, above gathers at neck front and at nose. Stuff legs, then body, then ladderstitch gap in seam.

Chest piece: Cut one pair of chest pieces from short-pile white fur fabric, using the cutting line shown on body front pattern. Join pieces at centre front edges. Pin chest piece to front of koala, matching centre front seams and neck edges. Sew raw edges to koala.

Face: Cut nose from black felt then pin it to face, with lower edge about 1·5 cm ($\frac{5}{8}$ in) above centre of mouth. Sew nose in place.

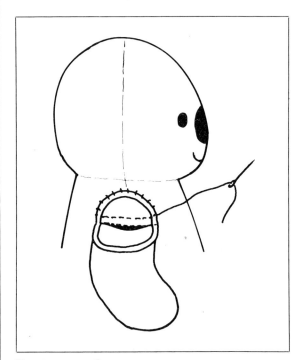

How to sew on the arms

Cut eyes from black felt. Trim off fur pile in a small circle around the marked centre of each eye. Glue eyes in position, pressing them firmly in place until glue dries. Trim fur pile slightly shorter below nose and above mouth.

Arms: Join arm pieces in pairs, leaving upper edges open between points C. Turn in seam allowance at open upper edges and tack. Turn arms right side out and stuff lower halves. Place an arm at each side of koala, with points D 2 cm ($\frac{3}{4}$ in) down from neck at side seams. Pin arm pieces which are nearest to body in place, then sew arms to body round upper edges and also backstitch them to body along the upper stitching line shown on arm pattern (*see diagram, opposite*). Stuff tops of arms very lightly then join upper edges.

Ears: Place ear pieces together in pairs then oversew raw edges together, leaving lower edges open. Turn right side out and oversew lower edges of each ear together, pulling stitches tightly to gather. If white fur pile is very long, trim it slightly. Sew ears to head front (see pattern on page 24 for position).

The clothes

Notes: 1 cm ($\frac{3}{8}$ in) turnings are allowed on all pieces unless otherwise stated. Draw patterns on to graph paper as for the koala patterns, marking on all details. Cut out fabric pieces as stated on patterns, noting any alterations in individual garment instructions.

Boy's dungarees

You will need: 30 cm ($\frac{3}{8}$ yd) of 91 cm (36 in) wide fabric; oddment of contrast fabric for pockets and binding; short lengths of narrow elastic; four small buttons; two snap fasteners.

To make dungarees: Join back pieces at centre back edges, stitching curve in seam twice to reinforce. Clip and trim seam at curve. Turn in waist edge 5 mm ($\frac{1}{4}$ in) then

1·3 cm ($\frac{1}{2}$ in) and stitch. Thread an 18 cm (7 in) length of elastic through this casing and secure it at each end.

Cut four pocket pieces from contrast fabric and join them in pairs, leaving a gap for turning. Trim seams and corners, then turn pockets right side out and slipstitch gaps. Sew pockets to positions shown on dungarees fronts. Join centre front edges of front pieces as for back pieces. Cut a 3 cm ($1\frac{1}{4}$ in) wide bias strip of contrast fabric. Sew one long edge to waist and bib edges of front on right side, taking a 5 mm ($\frac{1}{4}$ in) seam. Turn binding to wrong side, turn in raw edge 5 mm ($\frac{1}{4}$ in) and slipstitch to seam line.

Join front of dungarees to back at side edges. Hem ankle edges as for back waist edge and thread through elastic to fit ankles. Now bring centre front and back seams together and join inside leg edges of each leg, then clip seams.

For each shoulder strap cut a 4 by 24 cm ($1\frac{1}{2}$ by $9\frac{1}{2}$ in) strip of fabric. Join long edges and across one short edge of each strap, taking a 5 mm ($\frac{1}{4}$ in) seam. Trim seams and corners and turn straps right side out. Sew short raw edges of straps to inside waist edge at back of dungarees as shown on pattern. Sew snap fasteners to other ends of straps and inside top corners of bib. Sew buttons to pockets and to right side of bib at corners.

Girl's dress and panties

You will need: 40 cm ($\frac{1}{2}$ yd) of 91 cm (36 in) wide fabric; 1·60 m ($1\frac{3}{4}$ yd) of ric-rac braid; two snap fasteners; short lengths of narrow elastic.

To make the dress: Join dress bodice pieces round edges, leaving waist edges open. Trim seam and corners and turn bodice right side out.

For dress skirt cut a 12 by 91 cm ($4\frac{3}{4}$ by 36 in) strip of fabric. Sew on ric-rac 2·5 cm (1 in) away from one long edge (this will be hem edge of skirt). Join short edges of strip, taking a 2 cm ($\frac{3}{4}$ in) seam and leaving 7 cm ($2\frac{3}{4}$ in) open at waist end of seam, for back waist opening. Press seam to one side. Narrowly hem lower edge of skirt. Gather waist edge to fit lower edge of bodice and

sew it to one waist edge of bodice, with right sides facing, raw edges level and leaving other waist edge free. Turn in remaining waist edge and slipstitch it over seam.

For each shoulder strap cut a 4 by 13 cm ($1\frac{1}{2}$ by 5 in) strip of fabric. Make as for boy's dungarees straps. Put dress on koala and pin ends of straps at an angle, about 1 cm ($\frac{3}{8}$ in) inside top corners of bodice at front and back. Sew strap ends in place as pinned. Sew ric-rac round neck edges and over shoulder straps. Sew snap fasteners to back of bodice.

To make the panties: Use the dungarees back pattern for panties, cutting the lower edge along appropriate dotted line on pattern. Cut two pairs of pants pieces and join each pair at centre edges. Stitch curves in seams twice, then clip and trim the seams at the curves. Join the pairs to each other at side edges.

Hem waist and lower edges, taking 5 mm ($\frac{1}{4}$ in) then 1 cm ($\frac{3}{8}$ in) turnings to form casings for elastic. Thread elastic through to fit waist and legs, securing elastic at ends of casings. Bring centre seams together; join inside leg edges of each leg, then trim seam.

Cosy suits

You will need: 40 cm ($\frac{1}{2}$ yd) of 152 cm (60 in) wide Acrilan or Courtelle fleece (this will make two suits); oddment of contrast fabric for binding neck and sleeve edges; a 15 cm zip fastener for each; short lengths of narrow elastic.

Notes: Take care to cut the suit pieces having the 'most stretch' (usually across the width of the fabric) in the direction shown on pattern pieces. After cutting one pair of body pieces to pattern outline, trim off neck edge at dotted line on next pair for front pieces.

To make cosy suit: Cut four 11 cm ($4\frac{1}{4}$ in) lengths of elastic. Stitch elastic to wrong side of leg of each suit piece at dotted line shown on pattern, stretching elastic to fit as it is sewn.

Join the two front pieces at front edges between points E and F as shown on pattern. Turn in remainder of centre front edges and tack, then sew zip fastener to these edges, letting excess length of fastener extend above neck edges. Open zip fastener, then trim off excess length of zip level with neck edge of suit pieces. *Do not* close zip until suit is completed, to prevent the slide fastener slipping off.

Make a pocket from contrast fabric, in the same way as given for dungarees pockets. Sew pocket to left front at position shown on pattern. Join suit back pieces at centre back edges, from point E to neck edge. Now join front to back at shoulder edges. Join side edges and around lower leg edges as far as point E. Trim seams around lower leg edges.

Cut two bias strips of contrast fabric 5 by 19 cm (2 by $7\frac{1}{2}$ in). Sew one long edge of each strip to wrist edges of sleeves, with right sides facing, raw edges level and stretching bias slightly to fit wrist edges. Join underarm edges of sleeves. Turn bias to inside, turn in raw edges and slipstitch over seam. Sew armhole edges of sleeves to armholes of suit, matching point G to shoulder seams and matching underarm seams to side seams. Stitch armhole seams again close to first line of stitching, then trim seams close to this stitching line.

For the neck binding cut a 6 by 34 cm ($2\frac{3}{8}$ by $13\frac{1}{2}$ in) bias strip of contrast fabric. Bind neck edge in same way as for sleeves, letting

short ends of bias extend 1 cm ($\frac{3}{8}$ in) beyond centre front edges to allow for seaming. When turning bias to inside, turn in these short ends and slipstitch.

Boy's swimming shorts

You will need: Small piece of fabric; short lengths of bias binding and narrow elastic.

To make swimming shorts: Use the dungarees back pattern for the shorts, cutting the lower edge of pattern to the dotted line shown. Also trim 2 cm ($\frac{3}{4}$ in) off waist edge.

Join pairs of pieces at centre edges, stitching twice at curves to reinforce. Snip seam and trim at curves. Join the pairs to each other at side edges. Bind lower edges with bias. Hem waist edge and thread elastic through as for girl's panties. Now bring centre seams together and join inside leg edges of each leg, then trim seam.

Girl's bikini

You will need: 20 cm ($\frac{1}{4}$ yd) of 91 cm (36 in) wide fabric; 1·60 m ($1\frac{3}{4}$ yd) of narrow braid trimming; short lengths of narrow elastic; two snap fasteners.

To make panties: Make as for girl's panties, but trim 3 cm ($1\frac{1}{4}$ in) off waist edge of pattern before cutting out pieces. Sew trimming round waist edge stitching line.

To make top: Make top as for girl's dress bodice but join bodice pieces all round edges, leaving a gap for turning. Trim seams and corners, turn bodice right side out and slipstitch gap. Make and sew on straps as for girl's dress, using 4 by 11 cm ($1\frac{1}{2}$ by $4\frac{1}{4}$ in) strips of fabric. Sew trimming to lower edge, round top edges and over shoulders. Sew snap fasteners to back edges.

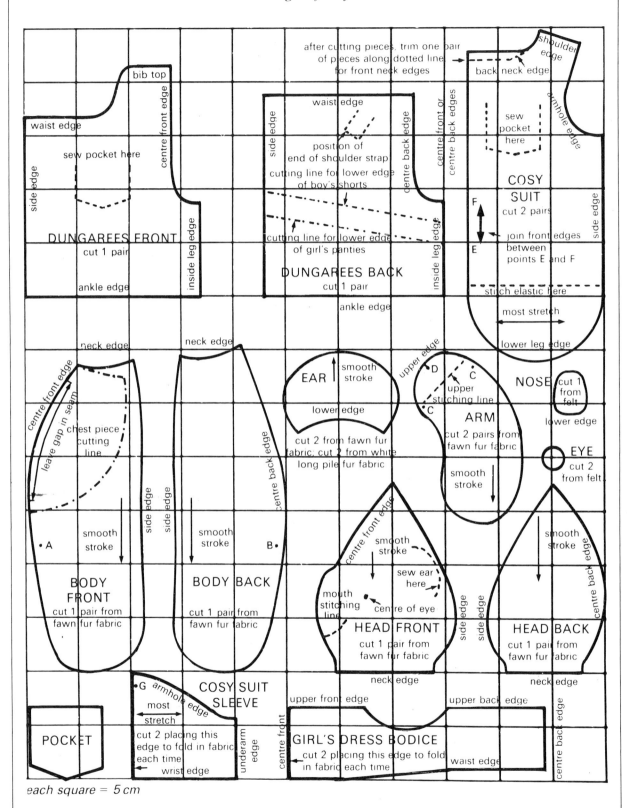

each square = 5 cm

Hippos

A whole family of cuddly hippos made in fur fabric from very simple shapes. Mother and Father hippo each measure about 38 cm (15 in) long, and the babies about 20 cm (8 in).

You will need: For each large hippo – 50 cm ($\frac{5}{8}$ yd) of 138 cm (54 in) wide fur fabric (note: this will make two large hippos if you follow the cutting layout); 350 g (12 oz) of stuffing; scraps of felt, shoe lace and ribbon; metric graph paper; adhesive. For each baby hippo – small pieces of fur fabric and a small amount of stuffing; scraps of felt and ribbon; metric graph paper; adhesive.

Patterns for large hippo: Fold the graph paper in half down the length. Copy body, leg, ear and tail outlines from the scaled down diagram on page 27 (each square on diagram = 2 cm) square by square on to graph paper. When drawing the patterns be sure to position the edges marked 'FOLD' against the fold in graph paper. Leaving the paper folded, cut out the patterns then open them out to full size. Cut neck dart out of body pattern along dotted stitching lines shown on pattern. Trace the full-size eye and nostril patterns off the page.

Patterns for baby hippo: To make a smaller hippo, each square on the diagram = 1 cm. Copy pattern outlines and cut neck dart out of body pattern in same way as for the large hippo. Trace the full-size eye and nostril patterns off the page.

Note: Seam allowances are as stated in instructions.

Large hippo

For the upper body, pin body pattern to wrong side of fur fabric following the cutting-out layout. Cut out upper body level with outer edge of pattern. Now use a marker pen to draw neck dart on to fabric level with cut edges of pattern. Draw centre

'fold' line on fabric, from each pointed end of dart. Remove pattern. Fold dart along fold line then stitch dart through stitching lines. Trim dart 1 cm ($\frac{3}{8}$ in) away from stitching line.

For under body, pin pattern to fabric, cut out and mark neck dart as for upper body. Now, leaving pattern pinned to fabric, trim pattern along underbody dart stitching lines. Mark this dart on to fabric in same way as for neck dart. Remove pattern and stitch neck dart first then trim dart 1 cm ($\frac{3}{8}$ in) away from stitching line. Stitch and trim under body dart in same way.

Now join upper body to under body all round outer edges taking a 1 cm ($\frac{3}{8}$ in) seam. Clip seam at curves. To turn body right side out, unpick a little of the underbody dart seam. Turn, then stuff firmly and ladder-stitch gap.

Cut eight leg pieces and join them in pairs taking a 1 cm (3 in) seam and leaving upper edges open. Clip seams at curves. Turn right side out and stuff legs then oversew top raw edges together. Sew tops of legs to body seam at positions illustrated. To keep legs in upright position, press them against body, then ladderstitch firmly to under body where they touch.

Cut out tail and oversew side edges together leaving top edges open. Turn right side out and oversew top raw edges together. Sew top of tail to centre back of body seam line.

Cut four ear pieces and trim fur pile a little shorter on each one. Oversew them together in pairs leaving lower edges open. Turn right side out then oversew lower edges together pulling stitches tightly to gather. Sew ears to head just in front of neck dart and 3 cm ($1\frac{1}{4}$ in) apart.

Cut blue or brown felt eyes and black pupils. Glue them together in pairs. Place eyes on head 2·5 cm (1 in) below ears and

2·5 cm (1 in) apart. Snip away fur pile beneath eyes, then stick eyes in place.

Cut nostrils from black felt and stick to head in same way as for eyes, placing them 2·5 cm (1 in) apart and 5·5 cm (2¼ in) below eyes. Cut a 6 cm (2⅜ in) strip of shoe lace for mouth and sew in place as illustrated. Snip fur pile a little shorter around mouth. Sew ribbon bow to top of mother hippo's head.

Baby hippo

Make in the same way as for the large hippo but trim darts to 5 mm (¼ in) from stitching lines and take 5 mm (¼ in) seams when joining body and leg pieces.

Sew ears to head just in front of neck dart and 1·5 cm (⅝ in) apart. Cut eye pieces and glue in place as for large hippo, positioning them 1·5 cm (⅝ in) apart and 1 cm (⅜ in) below ears. Cut nostrils and stick in place, positioning them 1 cm (⅜ in) apart and 2·5 cm (1 in) below eyes.

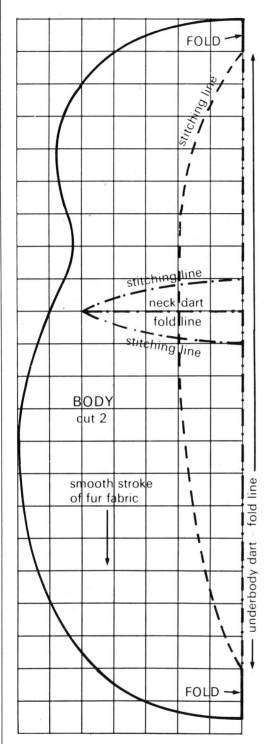

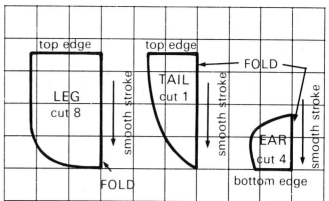

BODY
cut 2

smooth stroke
of fur fabric

For large hippo, each square = 2 cm
For small hippo, each square = 1 cm

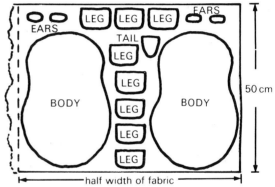

Diagram 1 Cutting-out layout for large hippos, showing how to cut two toys from 138 cm wide fabric

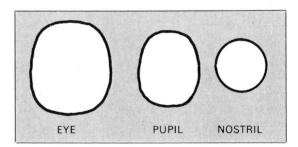

Diagram 2 Actual size patterns for large hippo's facial features

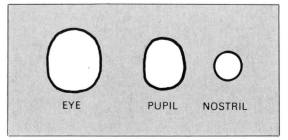

Diagram 3 Actual size patterns for small hippo's facial features

Farmyard Five

Soft, chubby and cuddlesome – these toys are easy to make, and they all come from one very simple body pattern. You can vary the shape of each animal by altering the pattern outline slightly. And you can adjust the size of each animal by drawing the patterns on to graph paper marked into 2 cm, 3 cm, 3·5 cm or 4 cm squares. If you want to make them smaller or larger, just copy the pattern on to smaller- or larger-squared graph paper.

Notes: To make patterns, over-rule your 1 cm graph paper into squares of the size mentioned in individual animal instructions, then copy patterns, following the outlines square by square, off the diagram on page 32 on to your over-ruled squares on the graph paper. Note that body outline variations for each animal are shown by dotted lines on the body pattern, and any variations are given in individual instructions. 5 mm ($\frac{1}{4}$ in) seams are allowed on all pieces unless stated otherwise.

Pig and piglet

For both toys you will need: 30 cm ($\frac{3}{8}$ yd) of 138 cm (54 in) wide pink fur fabric; 500 g (1 lb) of stuffing; small pieces of pink fleecy fabric or felt, deep pink felt and firm interfacing; strong thread for gathering; metric graph paper; a strand of deep pink double knitting yarn; adhesive.

The large pig

To make: (20 cm (8 in) high, and 25 cm (10 in) long). For pig patterns mark your graph paper into 3 cm squares, then draw patterns, noting that each square will represent 3 cm. For body pattern, draw *outline* of pattern, ignoring all the dotted lines.

Body: Cut one pair of body pieces from fur fabric. On each one, mark point A shown on pattern, with coloured thread, on right side of fabric. Join body pieces round edges, leaving back straight edges open. Turn body right side out and stuff firmly. Run a strong double gathering thread round back raw edges; pull up gathers tightly, leaving a finger-sized gap, then fasten off securely. Continue stuffing through gap if necessary. Now cut a 10 cm (4 in) diameter circle of fur fabric and turn in and tack raw edge. Sew circle to back of pig, with centre of circle placed over gap and with smooth stroke on circle going downwards.

Feet: Cut four 10 cm (4 in) diameter circles of fleece or felt. Gather each one round edge, stuffing firmly, then pull up gathers tightly and fasten off. Pin and sew feet under pig, with gathered edges against pig, placing them 1 cm ($\frac{3}{8}$ in) on each side of lower edge seam and with front and back feet 2·5 cm (1 in) apart.

Snout: Cut snout from two layers of interfacing glued together. Stick interfacing piece on to wrong side of pink fleece or felt, then cut this out 1 cm ($\frac{3}{8}$ in) larger all round than interfacing shape. Gather round raw edge and pull up gathers until fleece fits interfacing shape, then fasten off. Pin snout in place on pig, then use a darning needle to take a strong double thread from each marked point A through head to each centre point of nostril and back again, pulling thread tightly to depress nostril. Fasten off. Now sew snout in place round edge. Cut two 1 cm ($\frac{3}{8}$ in) diameter circles of deep pink felt for nostrils and glue them in place.

Mouth: Using pink double knitting yarn, secure yarn just above point A at one side of head, take it through to side of head below snout, then work two long stitches for mouth just below snout. Take thread back through head to just above other point A and fasten off. Trim fur pile shorter round mouth and snout.

Eyes: Cut two eyes from black felt and glue them on, with lower ends overlapping A.

Tail: Cut one pair of tail pieces from fleece or felt. Join them round edges, leaving short straight edges open. Trim seam, then turn tail right side out and stuff lightly. Sew open end of tail at centre back of pig, at top of fur fabric circle. Curl tail round and sew with a few stitches to hold curled shape.

Ears: Cut one pair of ear pieces from fur fabric, one pair from fleece or felt. Oversew a fur fabric ear to each fleece one, leaving inner edges open. Turn right side out and oversew inner edges together. Sew ears to head in a curve, about 4 cm (1½ in) up from eyes and 6 cm (2⅜ in) apart at top of head.

The piglet

To make: (14 cm (5½ in) high and 18 cm (7 in) long). For piglet patterns, mark graph paper into 2 cm squares, then copy patterns off diagram exactly as for pig, noting that each square on diagram will represent 2 cm.

Make piglet exactly as for pig, making the feet, and the fur fabric circle sewn to back, 7 cm (2¾ in) in diameter. Use 5 mm (¼ in) diameter circles for nostrils.

The sheep

You will need: 30 cm (⅜ yd) of 138 cm (54 in) wide cream curly fur fabric; 500 g (1 lb) of stuffing; small pieces of pale blue and black felt; strong thread for gathering; metric graph paper; strand of black double knitting yarn; adhesive.

To make: (23 cm (9 in) high, and 30 cm (11¾ in) long). For sheep patterns, mark graph paper into 3·5 cm squares, then draw patterns, noting that each square on diagram will represent 3·5 cm. For body pattern draw the outline, following upper and lower dotted lines for sheep marked on body pattern.

Body: Make body as for pig, but do not turn in raw edge of fur fabric circle before sewing it to back of sheep.

Feet: Cut four 12 cm (4¾ in) diameter circles of black felt and make as for pig's feet. Pin and sew feet under sheep, with gathered edges against sheep, placing them 1 cm (⅜ in) on each side of lower edge seam, with front and back feet 4 cm (1½ in) apart.

Nose and mouth: Cut nose from black felt and pin it in place. Using double black yarn, secure yarn under nose, then work a 2 cm (¾ in) straight stitch downwards, and a 2 cm (¾ in) straight stitch on each side of base of this stitch, to form a V-shape. Fasten off yarn under nose, then glue nose in place. Trim fur pile slightly shorter round mouth stitches.

Eyes: Cut two eyes from blue felt, then two pupils (shown by dotted line on eye pattern) from black felt. Stick pupils to eyes. Pin eyes in place, with centre lower edge of each eye at point A. Trim fur pile under each eye, then glue on eyes.

Tail: Cut two tail pieces from fur fabric. Oversew pieces together, leaving straight edges open. Turn right side out and oversew raw edges together, pulling stitches tightly to gather. Sew gathered edge to back of sheep at top edge of fur fabric circle. Catch lower end of tail to back of sheep.

Ears: Cut four ear pieces from fur fabric, trimming pattern along straight edge at line indicated. Make ears as for tail. Sew ears to head, about 4 cm (1½ in) up from eyes and 7 cm (2¾ in) apart at top of head.

The cow

You will need: 40 cm (½ yd) of 138 cm (54 in) wide golden-brown fur fabric; 500 g (1 lb) stuffing; small pieces of brown, black, pink and light fawn felt; small piece of long pile golden-brown fur fabric; strand of black double knitting yarn; strong thread for gathering; metric graph paper; adhesive.

To make: (27 cm (10½ in) high, and 36 cm (14¼ in) long). For cow patterns, mark graph paper into 4 cm squares, then draw patterns, noting that each square on diagram will represent 4 cm. For body pattern, draw the outline, following upper and lower dotted lines for cow marked on body pattern.

Body: Make body as for pig, using a 12 cm (4¾ in) diameter circle of fur fabric for back.

Feet: Cut four 13 cm (5 in) diameter circles of brown felt and make as for pig's feet. Pin and sew them under cow as for pig, but with front and back feet 8 cm (3 in) apart.

Tail: Cut a 5 by 8 cm (2 by 3 in) strip of fur fabric with smooth stroke going along length of strip. Oversew long edges together, then turn strip right side out. Sew one end of tail 2·5 cm (1 in) above top of circle at back of cow, with smooth stroke going downwards. For end of tail cut a 5 cm (2 in) square of long pile fur fabric. Make as for tail, and sew one end inside tail end. Gather up remaining raw edge.

Nostrils: Cut two nostrils from black felt. Glue them to cow as shown opposite.

Mouth: Using black yarn, work mouth as for pig, about 2·5 cm (1 in) below nostrils. Work mouth stitch four times before fastening off. Trim fur pile slightly shorter round mouth. Sew centre of mouth stitches to face with black thread.

Eyes: Cut two eyelids from pink felt, two eyelash pieces from black felt. Stick lower edges of eyelids to eyelashes, overlapping them 5 mm ($\frac{1}{4}$ in). Pin eyes to cow, with centre lower edges of eyelashes at points A. Trim fur pile under eyelids, then glue them in place, leaving eyelashes free.

Ears: Cut and make ears as for sheep's ears. Sew them to sides of head, about 8 cm (3 in) up from eyes and 10 cm (4 in) apart at the top of the cow's head.

Horns: Cut two horn pieces from fawn felt, placing edge of pattern indicated to fold in felt each time. Join pieces, leaving a gap in seam as shown on pattern. Trim seam and turn right side out. Stuff each horn as far as gap in seam. Oversew gap, then pin this centre unstuffed portion, flat on top of cow's head, so that horns are directly in front of ears. Sew them to head as pinned. Catch stuffed portion of each horn to head 2·5 cm (1 in) away from gap in seam.

To cover centre portion of horns, cut a 7 cm ($2\frac{3}{4}$ in) square of long pile fur fabric.

Turn in and tack the edge of square from which the fur pile strokes downwards. Sew this piece over centre of horns, so fur pile hangs down over the cow's face.

The dog

You will need: 30 cm ($\frac{3}{8}$ yd) of 138 cm (54 in) wide brown fur fabric; 250 g ($\frac{1}{2}$ lb) of stuffing; small pieces of black and blue felt; strong thread for gathering; metric graph paper; adhesive.

To make: (20 cm (8 in) high and 27 cm ($10\frac{1}{2}$ in) long). For dog patterns, mark graph paper into 3 cm squares, then draw patterns, noting that each square on diagram will represent 3 cm. For the body pattern, draw the outline, following the upper and lower dotted lines for dog which is marked on body pattern.

Body: Make body as for pig, using a 9 cm ($3\frac{1}{2}$ in) diameter circle of fur fabric for back of dog.

Feet: Cut four 9 cm ($3\frac{1}{2}$ in) diameter circles of fur fabric and make as for pig. Sew feet under dog as for sheep.

Nose: Cut nose from black felt. Gather and stuff, then sew nose in place.

Eyes: Make eyes as for sheep, but stick each pupil to one side of each eye.

Tail: Cut one tail piece from fur fabric. Fold it in half and oversew side edges together, leaving lower edge open. Turn right side out and stuff tail. Sew open end to back of dog, just above fur fabric circle.

Ears: Cut four ear pieces from fur fabric. Oversew them together in pairs, leaving lower edges open. Turn right side out and oversew remaining raw edges together. Sew ears to sides of head, about 6 cm ($2\frac{3}{8}$ in) up from eyes and 4 cm ($1\frac{1}{2}$ in) apart at top of head. Fold ears forward and catch them to head to hold them in place.

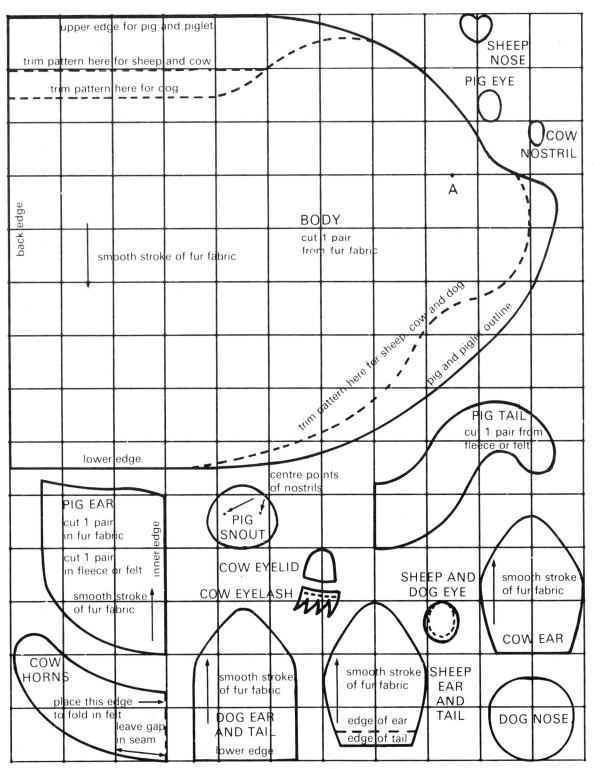

upper edge for pig and piglet

trim pattern here for sheep and cow

trim pattern here for dog

back edge

smooth stroke of fur fabric

BODY
cut 1 pair
from fur fabric

A

SHEEP NOSE

PIG EYE

COW NOSTRIL

trim pattern here for sheep, cow and dog

pig and piglet outline

lower edge

centre points
of nostrils

PIG TAIL
cut 1 pair from
fleece or felt

PIG EAR
cut 1 pair
in fur fabric

cut 1 pair
in fleece or felt

smooth stroke
of fur fabric

inner edge

PIG
SNOUT

COW EYELID

COW EYELASH

SHEEP AND
DOG EYE

smooth stroke
of fur fabric

COW EAR

COW
HORNS

place this edge
to fold in felt

leave gap
in seam

smooth stroke
of fur fabric

DOG EAR
AND TAIL

lower edge

smooth stroke
of fur fabric

edge of ear

edge of tail

SHEEP
EAR
AND
TAIL

DOG NOSE

Animal patterns *For piglet, each square = 2 cm   For sheep, each square = 3.5 cm*
For pig and dog, each square = 3 cm   For cow, each square = 4 cm

Penguin

A cheery soft toy penguin, about 40 cm (16 in) high. He's clad for warmth in jacket and bobble-cap (both sewn on as part of the toy), and he's delightfully simple to sew from fur fabric pieces – no patterns needed except for eyes and beak.

You will need: 40 cm (16 in) of 138 cm (54 in) wide black fur fabric (this will make two penguins); 20 cm (8 in) of similar width red fur fabric; 10 cm (4 in) of similar width green fur fabric; oddments of white fur fabric, printed fabric, tape or string, yellow, black and white felt; 500 g (1 lb) of stuffing.

Notes: When making penguin and garments make sure the smooth stroke of all fur fabric pieces goes downwards on the toy. Take 1 cm ($\frac{3}{8}$ in) seams unless otherwise stated.

Bind the edges of garments as follows: Cut 5 cm (2 in) wide straight strips of green fur fabric long enough to bind the required edge. Sew one long edge of binding in place on right side of garment, with raw edges level. Turn binding to wrong side and slipstitch other raw edge of binding over the seam line.

The penguin

For the body: Cut a strip of black fur fabric 40 by 46 cm (16 by 18 in), with smooth stroke running parallel to the short edges. Join short edges and note that this seam will be at centre back of penguin.

For base of penguin: Cut a 15 cm (6 in) diameter circle of black fur fabric. Sew it to lower edge of body. Turn body right side out and stuff, keeping base as flat as possible. Using strong thread and large stitches, gather round remaining raw edge. Pull up tightly and fasten off, oversewing to close completely. To shape neck, tie a length of tape or string very tightly round the body, 22 cm ($8\frac{3}{4}$ in) down from gathered top of head.

For white chest piece at front of body: Cut a 20 cm (8 in) square of white fur fabric. Sew raw edges of square to penguin at front, with one edge at neck and opposite edge turned just underneath base.

For tail: Cut two triangles of black fur fabric, measuring 15 cm (6 in) across the base by 7 cm ($2\frac{3}{4}$ in) high at apex. Join pieces leaving base edges open. Trim corners then turn right side out and stuff. Sew open edges of tail to back of penguin, with lower raw edge tucked under base, and upper raw edge against body.

To make foot pattern: Cut a piece of paper 10 by 12 cm (4 by $4\frac{3}{4}$ in). Round off corners at one long edge to form a continuous curved shape for outer edge of foot. To shape inner edge of foot, place straight edge of pattern just under penguin at front and draw curved shape of base on foot pattern. Trim pattern along this line. Cut four foot pieces from yellow felt using this pattern. Join them in pairs leaving inner curved edges open. Trim seam, turn right side out and stuff lightly, then stitch inner edges of each foot together close to edges. Now sew inner edges of feet to body just under base, level with edge of white fur fabric.

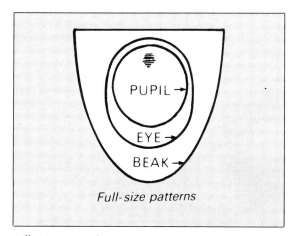

Full-size patterns

Full-size pattern for penguin's eye, pupil and beak

To make the face: Use the patterns on page 33 to cut two white felt eyes, two black felt pupils. Sew them together in pairs then work a highlight on each one with white stitches, as shown on pattern. Sew eyes in place, halfway down face and 2·5 cm (1 in) apart.

Use the pattern to cut two beak pieces in yellow felt; join them taking 3 mm ($\frac{1}{8}$ in) seam and leaving straight edges open. Turn right side out and stuff firmly, then sew beak to face below eyes as illustrated above.

The clothes

Jacket: Cut a strip of red fur fabric 15 by 50 cm (6 by 20 in). Round off the corners slightly at one long edge. Bind this edge and short edges with green fur fabric, easing binding round curves. Lay jacket aside for now.

For each sleeve cut a strip of red fur fabric 8 by 18 cm (3 by 7 in). Sew one edge of green fur fabric binding to one long edge of each strip, then join short edges. Turn binding to inside and sew in place.

Make a paper pattern for wing by cutting an 8 cm (3 in) square and rounding off corners at one edge. Cut four wings from black fur fabric. Join them in pairs, leaving straight edges open; turn them right side out. Slip a wing inside green binding of each sleeve, with raw edges of wings level with binding seam. Sew lower edge of binding to wing. Put a little stuffing inside each sleeve then oversew top edges together. Sew tops of sleeves to jacket, 3 cm (1$\frac{1}{4}$ in) below neck edge and 8 cm (3 in) within each green fur-trimmed short edge.

Run a strong gathering thread round neck edge of jacket. Place it around penguin's neck and tie ends of gathering thread tightly together at centre front. Space out gathers evenly, then sew jacket to penguin through gathers.

The cap: Cut a strip of red fur fabric 16 by 50 cm (6$\frac{1}{4}$ by 20 in). Bind one long edge, join short edges and complete binding as for sleeves. Gather remaining raw edge of cap with large stitches, then pull up tightly and fasten off. Gather and stuff a 12 cm (4$\frac{3}{4}$ in) diameter circle of white fur fabric and sew it to gathers. Place cap on head as illustrated and sew lower edge in place. Pull top of cap to one side and catch it in place.

Scarf: Cut a strip of printed fabric 10 by 66 cm (4 by 26 in). Join long edges and turn right side out. For the bobbles, gather and stuff two 6 cm (2$\frac{1}{4}$ in) diameter circles of white fur fabric and push each raw end of scarf inside before fastening off securely and sewing bobbles to scarf. Tie scarf round neck.

Cuddly Kitten

This soft furry kitten, with jaunty knitted hat and scarf, is about 35·5 cm (14 in) long from head to curled-up tail.

The kitten

You will need: 40 cm (16 in) of 138 cm (54 in) wide white polished fur fabric (*note:* if you buy 60 cm (24 in), you will have enough to make two kittens); 250 g ($\frac{1}{2}$ lb) of stuffing; a scrap of pink fur fabric or felt for the ear linings; scraps of black and pink felt for features; white button thread; oddment of grey double knitting yarn for marking paws; adhesive; metric graph paper; invisible sewing thread for whiskers (optional).

Note: 5 mm ($\frac{1}{4}$ in) seams are allowed on fur fabric pieces.

Patterns: Draw out the patterns on to graph paper, following the outlines on the diagram square by square. Each square = 2 cm. Mark all details on to pattern pieces.

Body: Cut two body pieces from fur fabric. Cut away the underbody dart, as shown on the pattern, in one body piece only. Join the raw edges of this dart, leaving a gap in stitching at centre, for turning. Now join body pieces all round edges. Clip corners then turn the body right side out. Stuff, then ladderstitch the gap in the dart.

Using double strand of grey double knitting yarn, work three stitches round end of each paw.

Head: Cut one pair of head pieces from fur fabric. Mark the mouth line on the wrong side of each piece, and also mark the eye point on the right side of each piece with a coloured thread.

Now machine stitch twice along each mouth line, with wrong side of fabric uppermost and using black thread. Join the head pieces, leaving neck edges open. Turn right side out and stuff firmly. Using double button thread, gather round neck edge. Pull up gathers to close neck edge completely, then fasten off. Trim fur pile above mouth lines, and at the end of the muzzle.

Glue two layers of pink felt together, then cut out nose using the full-sized pattern. Glue nose to end of muzzle.

Cut out eyes using the full-sized pattern. Use white thread to work a highlight on each eye as shown on the pattern. Place eyes on face, with top edges just below the coloured threads. Snip away the fur pile beneath each eye, then glue eyes in place. Snip off the coloured marking threads.

For whiskers, cut eight 25 cm (10 in) lengths of invisible sewing thread. Knot the lengths together at centre. Using a darning needle, take threads through the snout from one side to the other, pulling the threads until the knot catches. Knot threads at other side of snout, then trim whiskers to even lengths.

Place gathered edge of head on body at front, turning the head to one side. Hold the head in place with a couple of darning needles pushed into the head and body fabric. Ladderstitch head securely to body where they touch.

Cut one pair of ear pieces from white, and one pair from pink fur fabric. Oversew the ear pieces together in pairs, leaving lower edges open. Turn them right side out and oversew lower edges of each ear together, pulling stitches to gather slightly. Sew ears to head, setting them about 6 cm ($2\frac{3}{8}$ in) apart at top of head.

Cut one pair of tail pieces from fur fabric and oversew them together, leaving inner edges open. Turn tail right side out, using the knob of a knitting needle to push the end through, then stuff tail lightly. Sew inner edge of tail to centre back of underbody.

The hat and scarf

You will need: Two 20 g balls of double knitting yarn; a pair of No 9 ($3\frac{3}{4}$ mm) knitting needles; a cable needle.

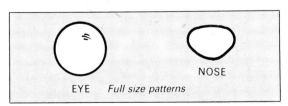

EYE   *Full size patterns*   NOSE

Full-size pattern for kitten's eyes and nose

Abbreviations: K, knit plain; p, purl; st, stitch; tog, together; cable 6 (slip next 3 sts on to cable needle and leave at front of work, k 3, then k 3 from cable needle).

Scarf

To make: Cast on 18 sts and work 6 rows in single rib. Work cable pattern as follows: *1st row:* (P 2, k 6) twice, p 2. *2nd row:* P. Repeat these 2 rows, twice more. *7th row:* (P 2, cable 6) twice, p 2. *8th row:* P. These 8 rows form the cable pattern. Work the 8 rows, 21 more times, then rows 1 to 4 again. Rib 5 rows, then cast off in rib.

Hat

To make: Cast on 80 sts and work 6 rows in single rib. Work cable pattern as follows: *1st row:* P 1, (k 6, p 2) to last 7 sts, k 6, p 1. *2nd row:* P. Repeat these 2 rows, twice more. *7th row:* P 1 (cable 6, p 2) to last 7 sts, cable 6, p 1). *8th row:* P. These 8 rows form the cable pattern. Work the 8 rows, 3 more times.
Next row: (K 2 tog) to end – 40 sts. Break off yarn leaving a long end. Thread yarn through sts, then pull up tightly and fasten off. Join row ends, then make a pompon and sew to top of hat.

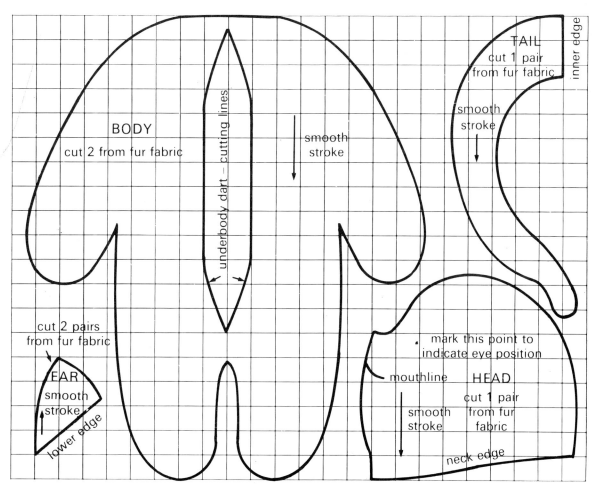

each square = 2 cm

37

2
SMALL
SOFT TOYS

Eight Sock Animals

Eight little animal characters – each one about 15 cm (6 in) tall (just the size to nestle into a child's hand), can all be made from stretchy towelling socks. You can make an owl, chick, penguin, mouse, teddy, pig, panda or a rabbit, using very simple pattern shapes.

You will need: Men's stretch towelling socks, size 6–11 shoe (one sock for each animal – note that panda and penguin will also need cuttings from another black or white sock); stuffing; oddments of felt, printed fabric and ribbon; adhesive.

To make each basic animal: (See also the additional instructions for some animals.) Use colours for animals as shown in illustration on pages 38–9. Turn the sock wrong side out.

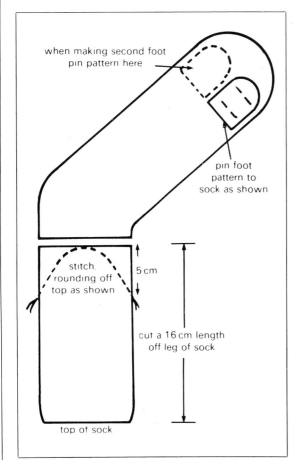

How to cut out the sock

Cut a 16 cm ($6\frac{1}{4}$ in) length off leg of sock for body and head of animal as shown in diagram (*below left*). Lay foot portion of sock aside until required later on. Stitch round cut edge of leg to form a pointed oval shape as shown in diagram (if you like, cut a piece of paper to this shape, pin it to sock and stitch close to edge of paper). Trim off corners of seam and turn right side out.

Stuff the animal so that it measures about 25 cm ($9\frac{3}{4}$ in) around. Run a gathering thread round remaining edge, pull up gathers tightly and fasten off securely. To form the neck, tie a strong thread tightly round body, 9 cm ($3\frac{1}{2}$ in) from top seamed edge. After knotting, sew thread ends into body.

Make all feet as follows: Cut foot pattern (the same for all the animals) from thin paper. Pin pattern to foot portion of sock, about 3 mm ($\frac{1}{8}$ in) from edge as shown in diagram. Stitch round close to edge of pattern, leaving straight edges indicated on pattern unstitched. Trim fabric level with straight edges of pattern, then remove the pattern and cut out foot close to stitching line.

Keeping the foot wrong side out, turn down raw edges 5 mm ($\frac{1}{4}$ in) and tack loosely. Turn foot right side out and stuff. For all animals except the penguin, owl and chick, make four feet and pin open edges of feet to animal at each side of body as shown in illustration on pages 38–9, then sew securely in place. For penguin, owl and chick, make two feet and oversew open edges of feet together. Place them in position at front of animal as shown, and sew in place.

For ears and wings use patterns as given for individual animals, referring to illustration for requirements. Sew ears and wings as for feet, but use one layer of sock fabric and one layer of printed fabric, placing them right sides facing. Turn down and tack raw edges as for feet then turn right side out. Oversew edges together, pulling stitches to gather slightly. Sew ears and wings to animals as shown in illustration.

Cut individual facial features from felt, using patterns, then glue them to face. Sew ribbon bows to animals.

Additional instructions

Rabbit: For tail, gather and stuff a 6 cm ($2\frac{3}{8}$ in) diameter circle of sock fabric and sew it to back of rabbit.

Penguin: Before sewing on feet and wings, add chest piece as follows: Cut a piece of white sock fabric 7 by 9 cm ($2\frac{3}{4}$ by $3\frac{1}{2}$ in). Round off corners at one short edge. Turn in all raw edges 5 mm ($\frac{1}{4}$ in) and tack. Sew chest to front of penguin, with short straight edge level with neck.

Mouse: For tail cut a strip off length of sock, 3 by 10 cm ($1\frac{1}{4}$ by 4 in). Fold and join long edges with a 5 mm ($\frac{1}{4}$ in) seam at one end, tapering to other end and rounding off this end also. Trim seam, turn tail right side out with a knitting needle then sew tail to back of mouse.

Pig: For tail cut a strip off length of sock, 4 by 16 cm ($1\frac{1}{2}$ by $6\frac{1}{4}$ in). Join long edges taking a 5 mm ($\frac{1}{4}$ in) seam and stretching the fabric as seam is stitched so that the tail will curl up. Round off one short edge also. Turn tail right side out with a knitting needle and sew it to back of pig. After sewing on ears, bend them forward and catch them to head.

Owl: Trim a little off lower edge of ear pattern as indicated, for owl. Do not gather the base of ears.

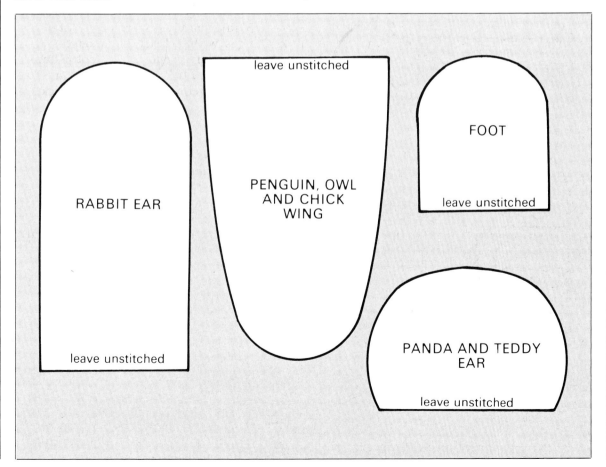

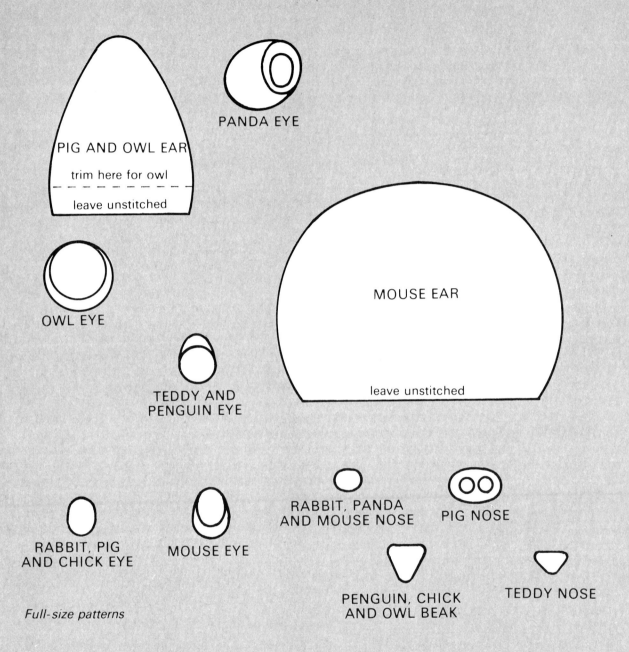

PANDA EYE

PIG AND OWL EAR

trim here for owl

leave unstitched

OWL EYE

MOUSE EAR

leave unstitched

TEDDY AND
PENGUIN EYE

RABBIT, PANDA
AND MOUSE NOSE

PIG NOSE

RABBIT, PIG
AND CHICK EYE

MOUSE EYE

PENGUIN, CHICK
AND OWL BEAK

TEDDY NOSE

Full-size patterns

Jungle Beanies

These miniature lion and tiger bean bags are just 9 cm (3½ in) in length. They are easy to make using the full-size patterns.

You will need: Small pieces of yellow and orange fleecy fabric; yellow fur fabric; felt; lentils for filling animal bodies (or they can be stuffed); stuffing for heads; permanent black marker pen; adhesive.

Lion

Trace tail, ear, eye and nose patterns off the page on page 44 on to writing paper and cut out. Trace off halved body pattern complete with all details on to folded writing paper, placing fold to dot-and-dash line on pattern and copying dart and gap stitching lines on to both halves; cut out folded pattern and open it out flat.

Pin body pattern on to two layers of yellow fleece, right sides facing. Stitch all round close to edge of pattern, leaving a gap in stitching at back of body as indicated. Before removing pattern, mark dart on one body piece. Remove pattern and cut out body

close to stitching line. Pull fabric layers apart and stitch dart as marked, then trim dart. Turn body right side out using the knob of a knitting needle to push through the narrow parts. Fill body with lentils using a paper funnel to help you. Ladderstitch gap in seam.

For head cut a 9 cm (3½ in) diameter circle of yellow fleece. Gather round edge then stuff. Pull up gathers tightly then fasten off.

For mane, cut a 9 cm (3½ in) diameter circle of yellow fur fabric. Turn in raw edge slightly and catch in place. Run a gathering thread round edge of mane then put head inside, gathered side down. Pull up gathers tightly round head and fasten off. Sew gathered edge to head.

Before working face, position head so that smooth stroke of fur fabric mane will be going away from forehead down back of head. For mouth work a vertical stitch in doubled black sewing thread, from centre of face downwards, then work a V-shape at base of stitch.

When glueing features in place, hold each on end of a pin to spread with glue, then position it on face. Cut nose from brown felt and stick in place. Cut black felt eyes (use a leather punch if available, to get perfect circles), and stick them in place.

Cut ears from felt to match body colour then sew lower edges to mane above face as shown in illustration on page 43.

Position head at front of body, turning it slightly to one side, and pin it in place. Ladderstitch head to body as pinned.

Cut tail from yellow fleece, using pattern. Bring long edges together, right side outside, and ladderstitch them together pulling stitches tightly to curve tail slightly. Push scrap of fur fabric inside narrow end of tail and sew it in place. Sew tail to back of lion.

Tiger

Make body as for lion, but using orange fleece. Use a black marker pen to mark stripes across body and legs as shown in illustration on page 43, blotting markings with a paper tissue as they are made, to press them into the surface of the fabric.

Trace off and cut out tiger head pattern (*below*) as for other pieces. Pin it to two layers of orange fleece, stitch, cut out and turn as for body. Work small stitches across base of each ear through both layers of fabric. Stuff head then ladderstitch gap. Make mouth, nose and eyes as for lion. Mark stripes on face as shown on face pattern. Sew head in place as for lion.

Make tail as for lion, marking on stripes before joining long edges; turn in end of tail and ladderstitch. Sew tail to back of tiger.

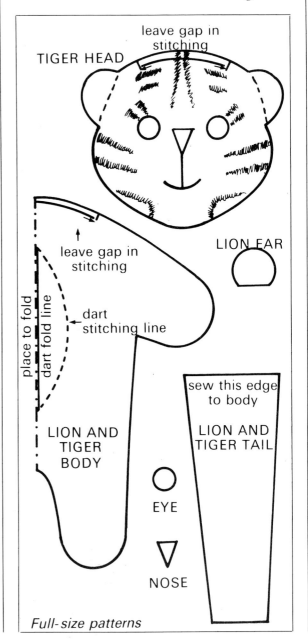

Full-size patterns

Four Small Animals

These four little animals, about 18 cm (7 in) high and 21·5 cm (8½ in) long from nose to tail, are all made from the same basic body pattern. Each one is given its individual characteristics by the addition of the appropriate eyes, nose, tail, etc.

You will need: Small pieces of fur fabric in colours illustrated on page 46; alternatively, 20 cm of 138 cm (8 in of 54 in) wide fur fabric will make two toys; small amount of stuffing; scraps of felt, ribbon, chunky knitting yarn; adhesive.

Notes: Trace all pattern shapes off pages 47–9 and mark on details. 5 mm (¼ in) seams are allowed on fur fabric pieces unless otherwise stated.

To make the basic body: Join body pieces together around head and back, from points A to B. Join underbody gusset pieces at upper edges from points A to B, leaving a gap in seam for turning. Now, matching points A and B, join one gusset to each body piece round legs. Turn body right side out and stuff firmly, then ladderstitch gap in gusset.

The lamb

Make basic body. For feet, cut eight foot pieces from felt. Join them in pairs, oversewing edges together and leaving upper edges open. Turn feet right side out and stretch felt slightly to make smooth, rounded shapes. Place a foot over each leg, pinning upper edges in place. Slipstitch upper edges to legs.

Join lamb's ear pieces, oversewing them together in pairs round edges and leaving lower edges open. Turn right side out. Fold ears in half at lower edges and oversew all raw edges together. Sew ears to lamb's head as shown in the illustration overleaf.

Fold tail, and oversew side edges together pulling stitches tightly to gather slightly. Then sew across end of tail. Turn tail right side out and sew to lamb as shown overleaf.

Trim fur pile a little shorter round end of lamb's face. Cut eyelids from pink felt, eyelashes and nose from black felt. Glue eyelids to eyelashes, overlapping lower edges of eyelids on to upper edges of lashes. Sew eyelids to lamb as shown in the illustration, leaving eyelashes free. Sew nose in place. Tie a length of ribbon in a bow around neck.

The bull

Make basic body. Make ears and feet and sew in place as for lamb. Cut eyes from blue felt, eyelids from pink and pupils from black felt. Glue them together as shown on eye pattern on page 47, then sew eyes to face. Trim fur pile a little shorter round end of face. Cut nose from pink felt and nostrils from black felt. Stick nostrils to nose, then sew nose in place. Cut tail from felt to match body colour and cut two tail end pieces from fur fabric. Oversew long edges of tail together. Oversew tail end pieces together, leaving upper edges open. Turn right side out. Slip lower edge of tail inside tail end piece and sew in place. Sew tail to bull.

Cut horns from white felt and oversew pieces together round edges leaving a gap in lower edge for turning. Turn right side out, stuff, then slipstitch gap. Sew centre of horns to head between ears. Cut horns' centre strip from fur fabric and place it over centre of horns. Sew front and back edges to bull's head and side edges to horns.

The donkey

Make basic body. Make feet and sew in place as for lamb. Make ears as for lamb using

45

donkey's ear pattern (*overleaf*), then sew them to head in upright position as shown in the illustration opposite. Trim fur pile a little shorter round end of face. Cut eyes from blue felt and pupils from black felt then stick pupils to eyes. Cut nostrils from pink felt, centre circles from black felt and stick them together. Sew eyes and nostrils in place.

For tail, wind yarn ten times around four fingers. Sew all these loops together at one end then sew to donkey. For the mane, make six more bunches of looped yarn in the same way as for tail. Sew two between ears to hang down towards face, then sew remaining four to head seam to hang down back on either side.

The dog

Make basic body. Oversew dog's tail pieces together, leaving lower edges open. Turn right side out, stuff, then sew tail in place.

Make ears as for lamb using dog's ear pattern (*overleaf*). Oversew upper raw edges of ears together then sew to dog as shown in the illustration opposite. Catch ears to head with a few small stitches about halfway down ears. Cut nose from black felt and run a gathering thread round edge. Stuff centre, pull up gathers tightly and fasten off. Cut eyes from blue felt and pupils from black felt and stick them together. Sew nose and eyes in place. Tie a length of ribbon in a bow around neck.

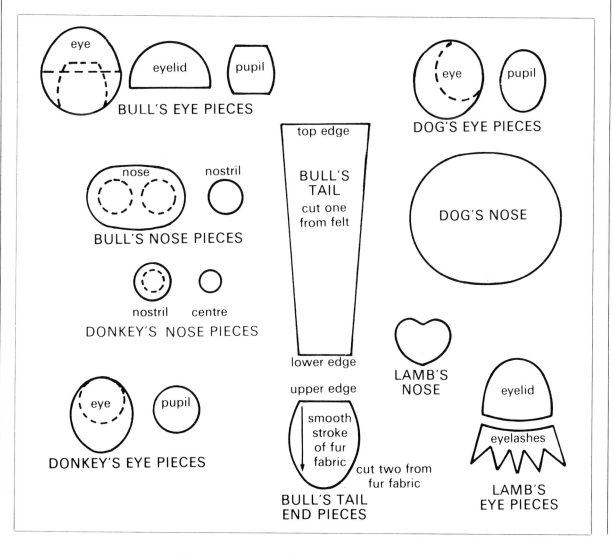

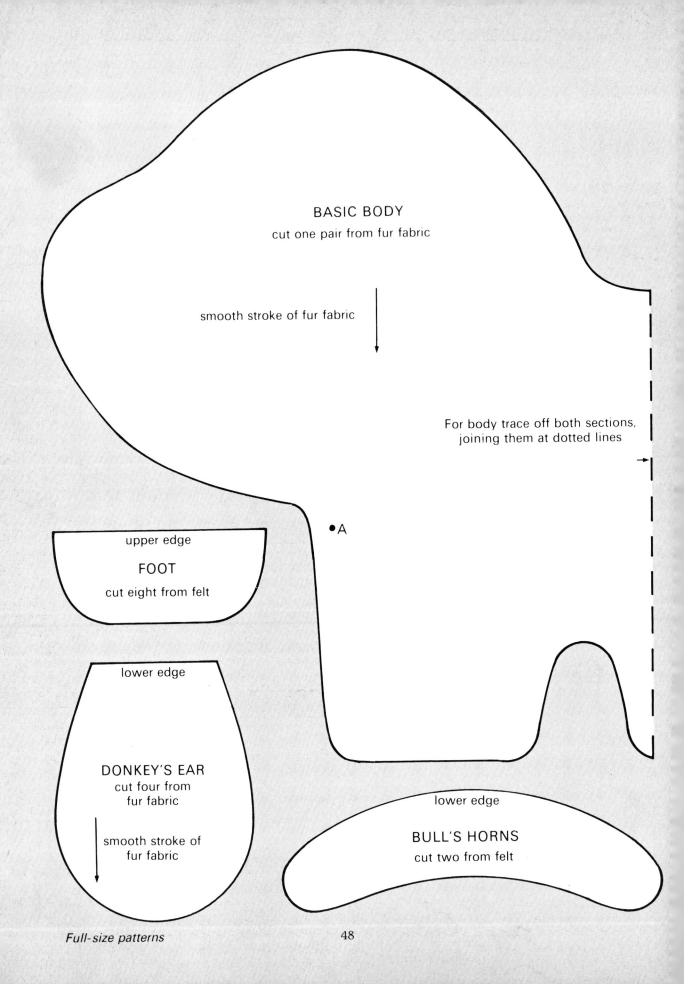

BASIC BODY
cut one pair from fur fabric

smooth stroke of fur fabric

For body trace off both sections,
joining them at dotted lines

•A

upper edge
FOOT
cut eight from felt

lower edge

DONKEY'S EAR
cut four from
fur fabric

smooth stroke of
fur fabric

lower edge
BULL'S HORNS
cut two from felt

Full-size patterns

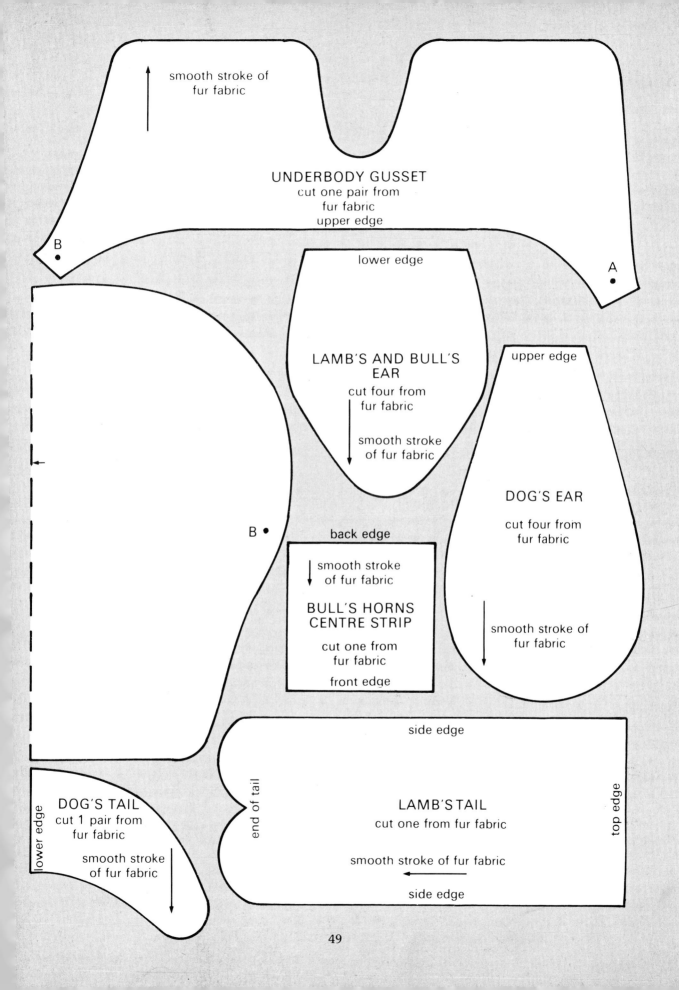

UNDERBODY GUSSET
cut one pair from
fur fabric
upper edge

smooth stroke of
fur fabric

lower edge

B

A

LAMB'S AND BULL'S
EAR

cut four from
fur fabric

smooth stroke
of fur fabric

upper edge

DOG'S EAR

cut four from
fur fabric

smooth stroke of
fur fabric

B

back edge

smooth stroke
of fur fabric

BULL'S HORNS
CENTRE STRIP

cut one from
fur fabric

front edge

side edge

end of tail

lower edge

DOG'S TAIL
cut 1 pair from
fur fabric

smooth stroke
of fur fabric

LAMB'S TAIL
cut one from fur fabric

smooth stroke of fur fabric

side edge

top edge

3
LARGE DOLLS

Football Mascot

This shock-headed football mascot is about 53 cm (21 in) tall. The actual colours of his shirt, shorts and socks are left to you – just pick the colours of your favourite team! The mascot itself should be made of felt; this is firm enough to give you a fairly rigid figure, but it will need dry-cleaning from time to time.

For the mascot you will need: 45 cm of 91 cm wide ($\frac{1}{2}$ yd of 36 in wide) flesh-coloured felt (or two 46 cm (18 in) squares); 450 g (1 lb) of stuffing; a small piece of fur fabric for hair; pieces cut off a pair of medium-size children's socks; a pair of black flat shoe-laces, small pieces of black and white felt, 5 mm ($\frac{1}{4}$ in) wide white tape and thin card for boots; scraps of black and pink felt, red embroidery thread and red pencil for face; adhesive; metric graph paper.

Notes: Copy all patterns from the diagram on page 55 square by square on to graph paper and mark on all details. Each square on diagram = 2 cm.

Before cutting out mascot pieces, test the stretch of your felt by pulling a small portion gently widthways then lengthways (the maximum stretch on felt is usually across the width – i.e. from selvedge to selvedge). Cut out all felt mascot and boot pieces with the maximum stretch across the width of patterns, as shown on each pattern piece. Mark darts and neck hole on back head piece, and all other points on pieces after cutting out.

Cut hair from fur fabric, with smooth stroke of fur in direction shown on patterns.

Stuff all parts of the mascot very firmly unless otherwise stated. Join all pieces with right sides facing and take 5 mm ($\frac{1}{4}$ in) seams unless otherwise stated.

The mascot

Cut two pairs of ear pieces and join them in pairs, leaving inner edges open. Trim seams and turn right side out. Stitch round ears, about 3 mm ($\frac{1}{8}$ in) away from seam. Cut front head piece then tack inner edges of ears to positions shown, with raw edges of felt level.

Cut back head piece and stitch darts as shown on pattern. Trim darts. Cut out neck hole as shown on pattern. Now join front head to back head, matching points A, leaving upper edges open and easing front head to the back between darts on back head. Leave head, wrong side out, for the time being.

Cut one pair of body back pieces and join them at centre back edges, taking a 1 cm ($\frac{3}{8}$ in) seam and leaving a gap in seam as shown on pattern. Cut one body front piece and join it to body back at side edges. Join body front to back at inside leg edges of each leg, squaring off seam at top as on pattern. Stitch again at this point to reinforce, then clip seam to corners. Turn body right side out through gap in centre back seam.

Now slip open upper edge of head down over body. Pull the neck edge of body through neck hole on back head piece, taking care to match points B and C. Tack neck edges together all round, then machine stitch the seam twice. Turn head right side out. Stuff head then run a strong gathering thread round upper edge. Pull up gathers tightly and fasten off. Stuff neck and body, then legs. Ladderstitch opening in body back seam.

The face: Cut nose from pink felt and stick it to centre of face, 5 cm (2 in) up from seam at lower edge of face. Cut eyes from black felt and work a highlight on each one with small white stitches. Stick eyes to face slightly higher up than the nose and 3.5 cm ($1\frac{3}{8}$ in) apart. Use red thread to backstitch an irregular W shape for mouth, 2 cm ($\frac{3}{4}$ in) below nose, then work back with the thread, oversewing through each back stitch. Colour cheeks by rubbing gently with red pencil.

The hair: Cut one front and one back hair piece. On back hair piece bring edges of each dart together and oversew. Oversew front hair to back hair along upper edges, matching points D and pulling stitches as you go to gather slightly. Turn hair right side out and place on doll's head. Sew face edge of front hair to doll, and also lower edge of back. Trim fur pile slightly shorter to neaten if necessary, at sides and lower back edge of head.

The football socks: Cut a 10 cm (4 in) section off leg of each sock, measuring from top of sock downwards. Turn over about 2 cm ($\frac{3}{4}$ in) at top edge of each piece, then slip socks on to mascot's legs, with raw edges of socks level with ankle edges of legs. Sew raw edges of socks to legs.

The football boots: Cut two pairs of boot pieces from black felt. Sew three strips of tape to each piece as shown on pattern, taking care to turn two of the boot pieces over when doing this, to make pairs.

Now join boot pieces in pairs at centre front and centre back edges, leaving a gap in front seam as shown on pattern. Clip seams at front as on pattern. Turn boots right side out then turn in upper edges 1 cm ($\frac{3}{8}$ in) and tack.

Cut two soles from thin card. Place one inside lower edge of each boot, matching points E and F. Glue 1 cm ($\frac{3}{8}$ in) at lower edge of each boot on to card soles all round. Place boots in position at ankle edges of legs, with the boots overlapping ankle edges about 1 cm ($\frac{3}{8}$ in) at back, and slightly higher at front. Pin boots in place, with toes of boots turned away from each other. Sew upper edges of boots securely to legs. Stuff ankles and boots firmly through gaps in front seams of boots. Slipstitch gaps in seams.

For the band around top edge of each boot, cut a strip of black felt 2 by 16 cm ($\frac{3}{4}$ by 6$\frac{1}{4}$ in). Fold each strip in half along its length then stitch long edges together. Glue strips around top edges of boots, oversewing short edges together at centre front.

For each boot cut another card sole and trim about 2 mm ($\frac{1}{16}$ in) off outer edges. Stick each card sole on to a piece of felt then cut out felt 1 cm ($\frac{3}{8}$ in) larger all round than soles. Turn and glue this surplus to other side of card. Glue card soles under boots.

For boot studs on the soles cut eight strips of white felt 5 mm by 10 cm ($\frac{1}{4}$ by 4 in). For the studs on the boot heels cut four 10 cm (4 in) strips of white felt, slightly wider than 5 mm ($\frac{1}{4}$ in). Spread each felt strip with glue then grip one end with tweezers and roll up tightly along the length. Glue four studs to each sole, and two heel studs to each heel (see pattern).

Cut two boot tongues from black felt and machine round each one, close to edge. Cut slits in each tongue as on pattern, then thread shoelace through slits and tie ends in a bow. Wind sticky tape round shoelace ends to seal. Sew tongues to tops of boots as shown in the illustration on pages 50–1.

The arms: Cut two pairs of arm pieces and join them in pairs, leaving upper edges open. Trim seams round hands then turn arms right side out. Stuff hands and thumbs lightly then machine stitch through hands along dotted lines shown on pattern. Pull thread ends through to one side of each hand, knot them, then sew thread ends into hands. Stuff arms to within 3 cm (1$\frac{1}{4}$ in) of upper edges. Bring seams together at top of each arm and oversew the edges together, pulling thread to gather slightly. Sew an arm securely to each shoulder at the position shown on body patterns.

The clothes

For the shirt you will need: 25 cm ($\frac{1}{4}$ yd) of 91 cm (36 in) wide fabric; cuttings off a lady's or man's knee sock; oddments of fabric as required to make the colours of your favourite football team.

For the shorts you will need: 15 cm (6 in) of 91 cm (36 in) wide fabric and a little elastic.

Notes: 1 cm ($\frac{3}{8}$ in) seams are allowed unless otherwise stated. After cutting out shirt and shorts pieces and before making up the garments, stitch on any side stripes to shorts, sleeve or chest stripes to shirt, as required for the particular club colours. Join fabric with right sides facing.

To make the shirt: Cut one pair of back pieces, one front and two sleeves. Join front to backs at shoulders. Clip armhole edges of front and backs at curves. Stitch armhole edges of sleeves to armhole edges of shirt, matching points G on sleeves to shoulder seams on shirt and easing sleeves to fit. Stitch seams again, just within first line of stitching, then trim seams.

Cut the sock open along length, down centre back and under foot to toe (*see diagram 1 below*). For each sleeve cuff cut a 7 cm ($2\frac{3}{4}$ in) wide strip across width of sock above the heel area (*see diagram 1*). Trim strips to about 15 cm (6 in) long if necessary. Stitch one long edge of each cuff to lower edge of sleeve, stretching cuff to fit and with raw edges level.

For neckband cut two 5 cm (2 in) wide

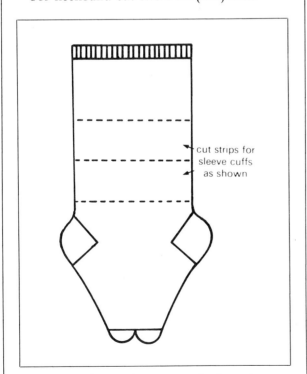

Diagram 1 Showing how to cut strips from a knee sock, for trimming football shirt

strips from sock as for cuffs. Join strips at one short edge, stitching seam as shown in diagram 2 (*below*), so that this seam will form the mitre at centre V-point of neckline. Trim seam.

Now clip V-point on shirt almost to seam allowance. Pin one edge of neckband V-point seam to front V-point of shirt. Pin remainder of neckband to neckline of shirt, with raw edges level and stretching band slightly as it is pinned. Trim off any excess length in band, level with centre back edges of shirt. Stitch band in place. Fold band in half to inside of shirt, then sew long raw edges of band together.

Join side seams of shirt and underarm edges of sleeves including cuffs. Clip seams at underarms. Trim seams on cuffs then fold cuffs in half to inside and sew raw edges together as for neckband.

Hem lower edge of shirt. Turn in one centre back edge of shirt 1 cm ($\frac{3}{8}$ in) and press. Put shirt on mascot with turned-in back edge overlapping the other back edge by 1 cm ($\frac{3}{8}$ in), and slipstitch neatly in place.

To make the shorts: Cut two shorts pieces and join them together at centre edges. Stitch again at curved portions of seams, then trim seams at curves. Bring centre seams together then join inside leg edges. Trim seams. Make narrow hems on lower leg edges. Hem waist edge, taking a 5 mm then 2 cm ($\frac{1}{4}$ in then $\frac{3}{4}$ in) turning. Stitch round close to fold in waist edge, thread elastic through casing to fit waist.

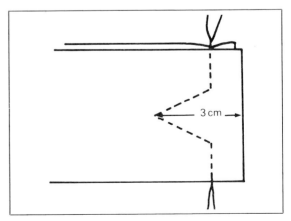

Diagram 2 Stitching the neckband seam to mitre the front point

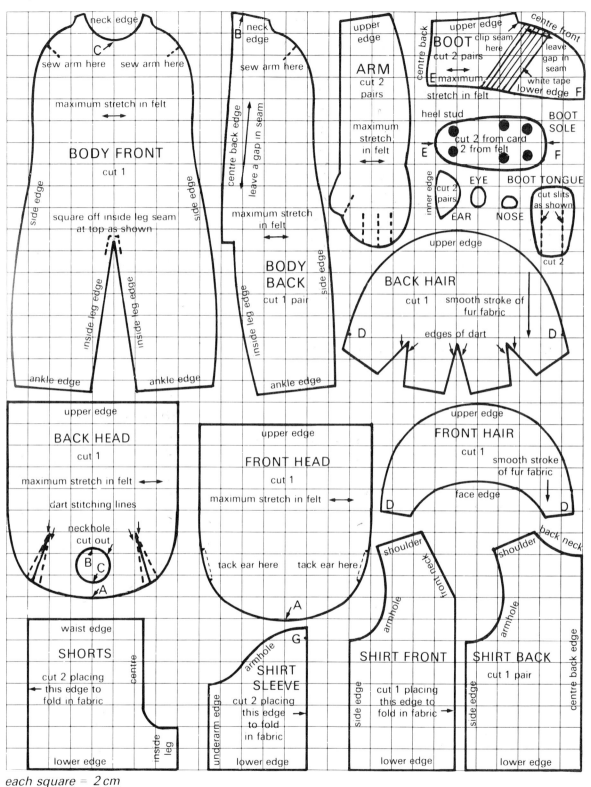

neck edge

C

sew arm here   sew arm here

maximum stretch in felt

BODY FRONT

cut 1

side edge

side edge

square off inside leg seam
at top as shown

inside leg edge

inside leg edge

ankle edge   ankle edge

B   neck edge

sew arm here

centre back edge

leave a gap in seam

maximum stretch
in felt

BODY BACK

cut 1 pair

side edge

inside leg edge

ankle edge

upper edge

ARM

cut 2
pairs

maximum
stretch
in felt

E

inner edge

cut 2
pairs

EAR

BOOT

centre back

cut 2 pairs

clip seam
here

E maximum

stretch in felt

centre front

leave
gap in
seam

white tape

lower edge   F

heel stud

cut 2 from card
2 from felt

E

**BOOT
SOLE**

F

EYE

NOSE

BOOT TONGUE

cut slits
as shown

cut 2

upper edge

BACK HAIR

cut 1   smooth stroke of
fur fabric

D   D

edges of dart

upper edge

BACK HEAD

cut 1

maximum stretch in felt

dart stitching lines

neckhole
cut out

B C

A

upper edge

FRONT HEAD

cut 1

maximum stretch in felt

tack ear here   tack ear here

A

upper edge

FRONT HAIR

cut 1

smooth stroke
of fur fabric

D   face edge   D

back neck

shoulder

front neck

armhole

shoulder

front neck

armhole

back neck

waist edge

SHORTS

cut 2 placing
this edge to
fold in fabric

centre

inside leg

lower edge

G

armhole

**SHIRT
SLEEVE**

cut 2 placing
this edge
to fold
in fabric

underarm edge

lower edge

SHIRT FRONT

cut 1 placing
this edge to
fold in fabric

side edge

lower edge

SHIRT BACK

cut 1 pair

side edge

centre back edge

lower edge

each square = 2 cm

55

Six Stretchy Dolls

A half-dozen colourful stretchy dolls about 26·5 cm (10½ in) in height, which are so easy to make from oddments of fabric. Their bodies, arms and legs are made from gathered circles, lightly stuffed, before threading on to elastic.

You will need: Oddments of fabrics (dress-weight cottons, etc. – which must be thin and soft enough to gather up tightly); 80 cm (32 in) of cord elastic, about 2 mm ($\frac{1}{16}$ in) in diameter, for each doll; pink or white cotton stockinette for heads and hands (or cuttings off an old plain T-shirt); small pieces of felt; small pieces of fur fabric for hair; oddments of braid and ribbon; stuffing; thin card for circle templates (cuttings off cereal packets, etc.); a red pencil for colouring cheeks; a bodkin with a large eye; adhesive.

Notes: 5 mm ($\frac{1}{4}$ in) seams and turnings are allowed unless otherwise stated. Follow basic instructions when making each doll, but refer to individual doll instructions before starting.

Basic doll

To make the gathered circles

Cut card templates in the following diameters: 10 cm (4 in), 11 cm ($4\frac{1}{4}$ in), 13 cm (5 in), 14 cm ($5\frac{1}{2}$ in), and 15 cm (6 in). Now referring to the table, cut out the number of circles stated in each size, by drawing round the templates on to fabric. Several circles can be cut at one time by pinning a few layers of fabric together. Cut bodice or shirt circles from one fabric and pants circles from another fabric, as shown in table and diagram, if the individual instructions say so.

Fold each circle into quarters and snip off the corner at the circle centre to form a tiny hole. Now turn in the raw edge of each circle 3 mm ($\frac{1}{8}$ in) and gather, taking 5 mm ($\frac{1}{4}$ in) long running stitches. Pull up gathers, stuffing the circle lightly, then pull up gathers as tightly as possible and fasten off.

To make the doll

For the head, cut a piece of stockinette 13 by 14 cm (5 by 5½ in), with the most stretch in stockinette going across the 14 cm (5½ in) measurement. Join short edges of fabric, then gather round one remaining raw edge, pull up gathers tightly and fasten off. Turn the head right side out.

For the body, cut a 50 cm (20 in) length of elastic. Fold it in half and knot the folded

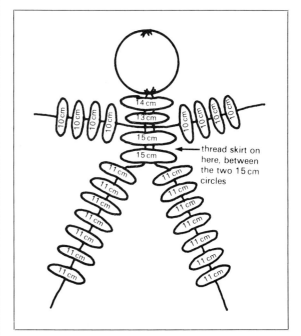

How to thread gathered circles on to elastics

TABLE
giving number of circles required
Cut these circles for bodice or shirt:—
EIGHT × 10 cm diameter
ONE × 13 cm diameter
ONE × 14 cm diameter
ONE × 15 cm diameter
Cut these circles for pants:—
ONE × 15 cm diameter
FOURTEEN × 11 cm diameter.

end. Stuff head to measure about 23 cm (9 in) around, then run a gathering thread round, 1 cm ($\frac{3}{8}$ in) away from remaining raw edge. Pull up gathers, turn in raw edges and enclose the knotted end of elastic. Fasten off gathers tightly, then oversew through elastic.

Now, referring to the diagram for the correct sizes, thread the first two gathered circles on to the doubled body elastic and push them up against the head. Cut a 30 cm ($11\frac{3}{4}$ in) length of elastic for the arms and pass this between the two body elastics. Continue threading circles on to the body elastics as shown in the diagram, noting position for threading on skirt for girl doll. Finally, thread arm circles on arm elastic.

Push all circles firmly together along each elastic, knot elastic and trim off excess.

Hands: Trace hand pattern off the page on to thin paper, then cut out. Pin the pattern on to two layers of stockinette, with most stretch in fabric in the direction shown on pattern. Trim fabric level with wrist edge of pattern. Now stitch all round, close to edge of pattern, leaving wrist edges open.

Remove pattern and cut out hand close to stitching line. Turn right side out and stuff. Gather wrist edge and insert knot at end of arm elastic, in same way as for head.

Shoes: Trace shoe pattern off the page as for hand. Pin pattern on to two layers of felt, then stitch all round close to edge of pattern. Mark the slit on to felt before removing pattern. Cut slit in this layer of felt only. Turn shoe right side out through slit, then stuff firmly.

Push knotted end of leg elastic inside the shoe at position of dot on pattern. Now ladderstitch edges of slit together, taking care to sew elastic securely to each shoe.

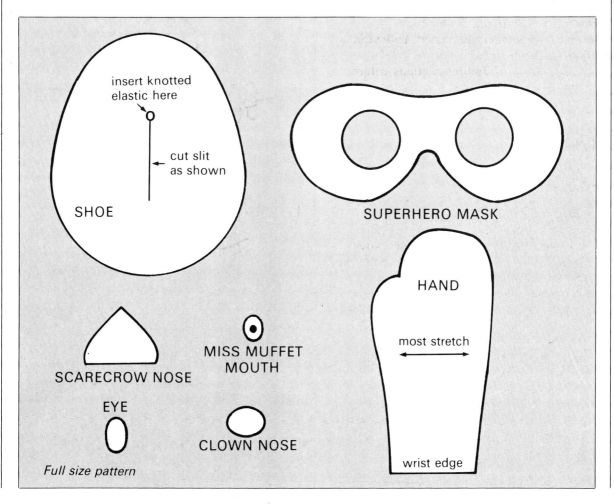

For face: Cut eyes from black felt and stick them in place half-way down face and 2 cm ($\frac{3}{4}$ in) apart. Work a V-shaped mouth, using four strands of red sewing thread, 1·5 cm ($\frac{5}{8}$ in) below eyes.

Colour the cheeks by rubbing them with red pencil.

For the nose, mark a red dot between the eyes of the doll.

The clown

Make the basic doll, using same fabric for all circles except for neck, wrist and ankle circles. Make these in a contrast colour.

Cut nose from red felt and glue it in place. Work a small black stitch above each eye for eyebrows.

For hair cut a strip of fur fabric 2·5 by 23 cm (1 by 9 in), with smooth stroke of fur pile going towards one long edge (this will be the face edge of hair). Oversew short edges of strip together. Turn in face edge of strip and catch it down. Place hair on head as shown in illustration (*right*) and sew both long edges to head.

For cap, cut a strip of fabric 12 by 26 cm ($4\frac{3}{4}$ by $10\frac{1}{4}$ in), to match body circles. Join short edges of strip. Turn in one long edge and press. Gather the remaining raw edge up tightly and fasten off. Turn cap right side out. Stuff top of cap lightly and sew turned-in edge to head, just overlapping hair. Gather and stuff a 6 cm ($2\frac{3}{8}$ in) diameter circle of contrast fabric, sew it to top of cap.

Make three more bobbles in the same way, using 3 cm ($1\frac{1}{4}$ in) diameter circles of fabric. Sew them to body circles at front of doll. Pull cap to one side and catch it to head.

The super hero

The super hero's suit looks most realistic made from ciré nylon fabric – silver for the main part of his body, contrasted with bright red for the details.

Make the basic doll, using same fabric for all circles except for neck and wrist circles

and the two circles at end of each leg. Make these in contrast colour. Make shoes to match these circles.

For hair, cut a 15 cm (6 in) diameter circle of fur fabric. Gather round edge and put hair on doll's head as shown in illustration (*below*) with smooth stroke of fur fabric going from back of neck towards forehead. Pull up gathers to fit head and fasten off. Sew gathered edge to head.

For the cape, cut two pieces of fabric 14 by 20 cm ($5\frac{1}{2}$ by 8 in), to match contrast circles. Join them, leaving a gap in seam for turning. Turn right side out and slipstitch gap. Gather one long edge and secure gathering thread round the elastic below the head.

Cut mask from felt and glue it to face.

The cowboy

Make the basic doll, using checked fabric for shirt circles and blue fabric for pants circles. Make hair as for super hero.

For the neckerchief, cut a 17 cm ($6\frac{3}{4}$ in) square of fabric. Fray out edges then fold into a triangle and tie round elastic below head.

For hat brim, cut a 15 cm (6 in) diameter circle of paper, then cut a 9 cm (3½ in) diameter circle from the centre. Pin brim pattern on to two layers of felt. Stitch all round, close to outer and inner edges of pattern. Remove pattern and cut out brim close to stitching lines.

For hat crown, cut two pieces of felt 8 by 14 cm (3 by 5½ in), to match brim. Round off one long edge of each piece to form a semi-circle. Stitch pieces together round curve. Trim seam and turn right side out. Oversew straight edges of crown to inner edge of brim.

Stuff top of hat, place it on head and sew it to head round lower edge of crown. Glue braid round for hatband. Indent crown at top and sides, then catch it to head at these positions. Turn up brim at front and back and catch to crown.

The scarecrow

Make the basic doll, using one fabric for shirt circles and another for pants circles. Before threading circles on to elastic, sew on a few coloured fabric patches. Patch the shoes and darn hands also.

Cut nose from orange felt and oversew side edges together. Stuff nose and sew it to face. For hair, cut a strip of coarsely woven yellow fabric, 10 by 24 cm (4 by 9½ in). Fray out both long edges, leaving a 2 cm (¾ in) portion at centre of strip unfrayed. (*Note:* keep the frayed-out strands until later on.) Fold hair strip, bringing long frayed-out edges together, and sew the folded edge round head. Trim strands short above eyes.

Now, using the frayed-out strands, knot a few here and there round body and leg elastics between the circles, and trim ends.

Make hat and sew it in place as for cowboy hat, using tweedy fabric and the following sizes: For brim, a 12 cm (4¾ in) diameter circle with a 7 cm (2¾ in) circle at centre; for crown, two 7 by 13 cm (2¾ by 5 in) pieces, rounding off one long edge of each. For scarf, cut a strip of fabric 6 by 24 cm (2¼ by 9½ in). Fray out edges and knot scarf round elastic below head.

Miss Muffet

Make skirt first. Cut a strip of fabric 14 by 50 cm (5½ by 20 in), and join short edges. Narrowly hem one long raw edge and sew on braid above hem. Gather remaining long raw edge up tightly and fasten off.

Now make basic doll, using same fabric as skirt for bodice, except for neck and wrist circles. Make these in contrast colour.

Make pants circles in a different fabric. Thread on skirt at position shown on diagram.

Cut mouth from red felt and mark black dot at centre. Stick mouth in place. Make hair and sew it in place as for super hero, but use a 16 cm (6¼ in) diameter circle of fur fabric. Sew ribbon bow to hair.

For the spider, gather and stuff a 4 cm (1½ in) diameter circle of black fabric. To make the legs, use double black thread and sew four short loops at each side of spider. Spread loops with a little glue and smooth the strands of thread together. Trim legs to even lengths. Work two white stitches for eyes. Sew spider to the skirt.

Cinderella

Make skirt first as for Miss Muffet, and sew on patches of fabric as shown in illustration. Make basic doll and hair as for Miss Muffet but work a small inverted V-shape for mouth.

For the broom, cut a strip of brown tweedy fabric 9 by 16 cm (3½ by 6¼ in) and fray out 5 cm (2 in) at one short edge. Now roll up fabric strip very tightly across the width, then wind strong thread tightly round and round to make a firm handle, leaving frayed-out strands unbound. Sew the thread ends into the handle, then sew the broom handle to Cinderella's right hand.

Jennifer Rag Doll

Jennifer is a big armful of a rag doll – about 61 cm (24 in) tall. She is made from cotton stockinette with yarn hair divided into ten plaits. She also has lots of removable clothes – pantaloons and petticoat, dress, apron and mob cap.

For the doll you will need: 50 cm ($\frac{5}{8}$ yd) of pink cotton stockinette – tubular knit 57 cm ($22\frac{1}{2}$ in) wide, opening out to 114 cm (45 in) width; 600 g ($1\frac{1}{4}$ lb) of stuffing; one 50 g ball of double knitting yarn for hair; short length of tape for joining hair to head; two black trouser-type buttons, about 2 cm ($\frac{3}{4}$ in) in diameter, for eyes (or if doll is for a very young child, use circles of black felt); strong black and pink thread; red pencil for colouring cheeks; pieces of felt, narrow ric-rac braid, and ribbon for shoes; red, pink, black embroidery thread; metric graph paper; adhesive.

Notes: Copy all patterns from the diagrams on pages 65–6, square by square, on to graph paper, and mark on all details. Each square on diagram = 5 cm. For body and head pieces, draw pattern for back of doll following outline, then draw pattern again for front and trim pattern along centre back dotted line as indicated.

Take care to cut out stockinette pieces with most stretch in fabric going in the direction shown on each pattern. Take 5 mm ($\frac{1}{4}$ in) seams unless stated otherwise. Use a small machine stitch when sewing stockinette, and stretch the fabric slightly as it is stitched, so seams will not snap when pieces are stuffed.

The doll

Body and head

Cut one pair of back pieces and mark dots on right side of fabric for position of eyes. Join pieces at centre back edges, taking a 1 cm ($\frac{3}{8}$ in) seam and leaving a gap in seam as indicated. Cut one front piece, placing edge indicated to fold in fabric. Mark dots on right side of fabric for eye positions and corners of mouth.

Join front to back, right sides facing, all round edges. Clip seam at neck and trim seam round lower corners of body. Turn right side out through back opening.

Stuff head, neck and body very firmly, then ladderstitch gap in seam. (When stuffed, the head should measure about 39 cm ($15\frac{1}{2}$ in) around, and the body about 37 cm ($14\frac{1}{2}$ in) around.) Tie four strands of strong pink thread round neck, pulling and knotting threads tightly at back of doll to shape neck. Sew thread ends into neck.

To sew on buttons for eyes, use a long darning needle and doubled strong black thread. Take threads through from dot at back of head to dot at front. Thread on button through one pair of holes, with upper surface of each button against face. Take thread through to back of head again and knot threads tightly to depress button into face. Repeat once more through remaining pair of holes in button. Lift button carefully away from face, and spread a little glue underneath to fix eyes firmly to face.

Indent corners of mouth as for eyes, using darning needle, single strong pink thread, and taking threads through from back of head near positions of eye threads.

Colour cheeks by rubbing fabric with the *side* (not the point) of the red pencil. Mark on eyelashes and also a shallow U-shape between indented corners of mouth. Mark on nose as shown in illustration on page 62.

When embroidering facial features which follow, start and fasten off embroidery threads at back of head. Take the threads through to face with a long darning needle, use an ordinary needle to work the stitches, then pass threads through to back of head with darning needle again. Work small back stitches in red for mouth, then work oversewing stitches through each back stitch. Work the nose in the same way, using pink, then work straight black stitches for eyelashes.

Legs and shoes

Cut two leg pieces, placing edge of pattern indicated to fold in fabric each time. Cut two pairs of shoe pieces and two soles from felt. Join centre front edges of shoe pieces and trim seams. Now stitch ankle edges of legs to upper edges of shoes, with right sides facing, raw edges level and stretching stockinette to fit edges of felt. Join centre back edges of legs and shoes and trim seams. Tack, then stitch soles to shoes, matching points A and B. Trim seams.

Turn legs right side out and stuff firmly. Turn in top edges and oversew, with leg seams at centre back of legs. Sew ric-rac round top edges of shoes and sew ribbon bows to fronts of shoes. Sew legs securely to lower edge of body.

Arms

Cut out arms as for legs. Stitch seams then turn and stuff to within 3 cm ($1\frac{1}{4}$ in) of top edges. Turn in top edges and oversew, with each arm seam at underarm, pulling stitches tightly to gather. Tie strong pink thread tightly round each arm, 6 cm ($2\frac{3}{8}$ in) from ends, to shape wrists, then sew thread ends into arms. Sew ar   to sides of body, 3 cm ($1\frac{1}{4}$ in) down from neck.

Hair

For fringe, wind a strand of yarn twenty times round an 8 cm (3 in) piece of card. Slip yarn off card and sew loops together at one end. Sew fringe to top of head to hang down over forehead.

For hair, cut remaining yarn into 70 cm (28 in) lengths. Keep aside a few lengths for knotting round ends of plaits. Now stitch centres of yarn to a 20 cm (8 in) length of tape, keeping yarn 1 cm ($\frac{3}{8}$ in) within each end of tape. Turn in ends of tape then sew hair, tape side down, to centre parting position on head, starting about 6 cm ($2\frac{3}{8}$ in)

above eyes. Now smooth all the yarn strands down sides and back of head, then tie a length of tape round head, level with eyes, to hold strands in place.

Divide strands at each side of head into five roughly equal sections. Plait each section below the tape, making plaits of equal length. Knot strands of yarn round ends of plaits. Remove the tape, then catch each plait to head with small stitches taken through tops of plaits and into head. Trim yarn ends to even lengths on all plaits.

The clothes

Notes: Take 1 cm ($\frac{3}{8}$ in) seams and turnings on all pieces, unless stated otherwise. Join fabric with right sides facing unless other instructions are given.

Pantaloons and petticoat

You will need: 90 cm (1 yd) of 91 cm (36 in) wide fabric; short lengths of narrow elastic; 60 cm (24 in) strip of narrow ribbon or tape for the elastic casing on legs of pantaloons; 6 m ($6\frac{5}{8}$ yd) of narrow frilled lace edging; three snap fasteners.

To make pantaloons: Cut two pieces, placing edge of pattern indicated to fold in fabric each time. Narrowly hem lower edges of each piece and sew on lace edging, then sew another row of lace edging above first row. Sew ribbon or tape to wrong side of each piece, as shown by dotted lines on pattern. Thread elastic through to fit legs and secure it at each side of casing with a few stitches.

Now join pieces to each other at centre edges, stitching twice at curved parts of seams to reinforce. Trim seams at curves. Bring centre seams together and stitch inside leg seams on each leg. Turn pantaloons right side out and hem waist edge, taking 1 cm ($\frac{3}{8}$ in) turnings twice. Thread elastic through to fit doll's waist.

To make petticoat: Cut bodice front, placing dotted line shown on pattern to fold in

fabric. Cut one pair of back pieces to pattern outline. Turn in shoulder edges of each piece and press. Join front to backs at side edges and trim seams. Make a lining for bodice from same fabric in same way.

Join lining to bodice round neck, armhole and centre back edges. Trim seams and clip curves. Turn bodice right side out, then slip stitch front shoulder edges of bodice to back shoulder edges. Join shoulder edges of lining in same way. Press bodice, then sew lace edging round armholes and neck edge.

For petticoat skirt, cut a strip of fabric 18 by 91 cm (7 by 36 in), then cut two strips 10 by 91 cm (4 by 36 in) for skirt frill. Cut one frill strip in half across width, and join one short end of each half to ends of the other frill strip. Narrowly hem one long edge of frill and sew on two rows of lace edging as for pantaloons. Gather remaining long raw edge of frill strip to fit one long edge of skirt, then sew it in place, right sides facing and raw edges level. Join short edges of skirt, from frilled hem to within 10 cm (4 in) of waist edge. Neaten open edges for back opening of skirt.

Gather waist edge of skirt to fit lower edge of petticoat bodice. Sew it to bodice, right sides facing, raw edges level and leaving bodice lining free. Turn in lower edge of lining and slipstitch it over seam.

Sew lace edging round petticoat at waist seam, then sew snap fasteners to centre back edges of bodice.

The dress

You will need: 80 cm ($\frac{7}{8}$ yd) of 91 cm (36 in) wide printed fabric; 3 m ($3\frac{3}{8}$ yd) of broderie anglaise lace edging; 2 m ($2\frac{1}{4}$ yd) of wide ric-rac braid; 70 cm (28 in) of narrow ric-rac braid; four snap fasteners.

To make dress: For the skirt cut two strips of fabric 25 by 91 cm (10 by 36 in). Cut one strip in half across width and join one end of each half to an end of long strip. Stitch top of lace edging to skirt, about 5 cm (2 in) above one long edge (this is the hem edge of skirt). Sew wide ric-rac to top edge of lace. Now join short edges of skirt, from hem edge to within 10 cm (4 in) of waist edge. Press

seam to one side and neaten raw edges of opening. Narrowly hem lower edge of skirt.

Cut bodice front, placing dotted line shown on pattern to fold in fabric. Cut one pair of backs to pattern outline. Join front to backs at shoulder edges. Turn in centre back edges of bodice 1 cm ($\frac{3}{8}$ in) twice and stitch in place.

Cut a 50 cm (19$\frac{1}{2}$ in) length of lace edging and neaten ends. Gather it to fit round neck of bodice, then sew raw edge to raw edge of neck, with right sides of both uppermost and raw edges level. Now bind neck edge of bodice with a 4 cm (1$\frac{1}{2}$ in) wide bias strip of fabric, trimming seam before sewing second edge of binding in place. Sew narrow ric-rac to bias, next to lace edging.

Join dress front to backs at side edges. Cut two dress sleeves, placing pattern to fold in fabric each time. Run gathering threads between dots at shoulder edges of sleeves. Join underarm edges of sleeves. Tack shoulder edges of sleeves into armholes of bodice, matching underarm seams to side seams and pulling up gathers to fit bodice armholes. Stitch seams twice. Trim seams.

For each wrist frill, cut a 35 cm (13$\frac{1}{2}$ in) strip of lace edging. Join ends of each, then gather to fit wrist edges of sleeves. Sew gathered edges of lace to wrist edges of sleeves, with right sides facing and raw edges level.

Bind these raw edges with 3 cm (1$\frac{1}{4}$ in) wide bias strips of fabric, turning bias completely to wrong side when sewing second edge in place. Sew narrow ric-rac above frills.

Gather waist edge of skirt to fit lower edge of bodice, then sew it in place. Sew snap fasteners to back edges of bodice.

The apron

You will need: 60 cm ($\frac{3}{4}$ yd) of 91 cm (36 in) wide fabric; 3 m ($3\frac{3}{8}$ yd) of ric-rac braid; two hooks and eyes; four small buttons.

To make apron: Cut one apron bodice back, placing edge indicated to fold in fabric. Cut one pair of bodice fronts. Join fronts to back at side and shoulder edges. Make another bodice for lining in same way. Join bodice to lining at centre front and around neck edges. Trim seams and clip curves and corners. Turn right side out. Tack armhole edges together.

Cut two apron sleeves, placing edge shown on pattern to fold in fabric each time. Take narrow hems on lower edges of sleeves, then sew on ric-rac. Join underarm edges of sleeves. Run gathering threads all round shoulder edges of sleeves, then pull up gathers to fit bodice armholes. Sew sleeves in place, matching underarm seams to side seams of bodice, and matching dots on sleeves to shoulder seams of bodice. Trim seams and neaten raw edges. Hand-sew ric-rac up fronts of bodice and around neck, taking care not to catch lining to bodice at centre front edges.

For apron skirt, cut two strips of fabric 18 by 60 cm (7 by 24 in). Join them at one short edge, for centre back seam of skirt. At remaining short edges, cut a generous curve from one long edge round on to short edges (this will be hem edge of skirt). Narrowly hem this long edge, round curves and up short edges. Sew on ric-rac as shown on illustration on front cover.

Gather remaining long raw edge of skirt to fit lower edge of bodice. Sew gathered edge to bodice, right sides facing, raw edges level and leaving bodice lining free. Turn in lower raw edge of bodice lining and slipstitch it over seam. Sew ric-rac round waist edge of bodice, then sew hooks and eyes to front edges and sew on buttons as shown on illustration on front cover.

Mob cap

You will need: A strip of fabric 38 by 82 cm (15 by $32\frac{1}{2}$ in); 1 m ($1\frac{1}{8}$ yd) of narrow ric-rac braid; short length of elastic; scrap of fabric or felt to match ric-rac, and a little stuffing; ribbon for bow.

To make mob cap: Fold fabric strip in half down length, right side out, and press folded edge. Open up again and stitch ric-rac about 1 cm ($\frac{3}{8}$ in) away from pressed fold. Join short edges of strip for centre back seam. Fold strip in half down length as before, and tack long edges together.

For elastic casing, run a line of stitching round cap, about 4 cm ($1\frac{1}{2}$ in) above ric-rac, then stitch again 1 cm ($\frac{3}{8}$ in) above first line of stitching. On inside of cap, unpick centre back seam between stitching lines for elastic casing, then thread elastic through to fit doll's head, and slipstitch seam again.

Run a gathering thread round remaining top raw edges of cap, pulling up gathers tightly until raw edges touch. Fasten off. To cover these raw edges, gather and stuff an 8 cm (3 in) diameter circle of fabric to match ric-rac. Sew this to top of cap to cover gathered raw edges. Sew ribbon bow to front of mob cap.

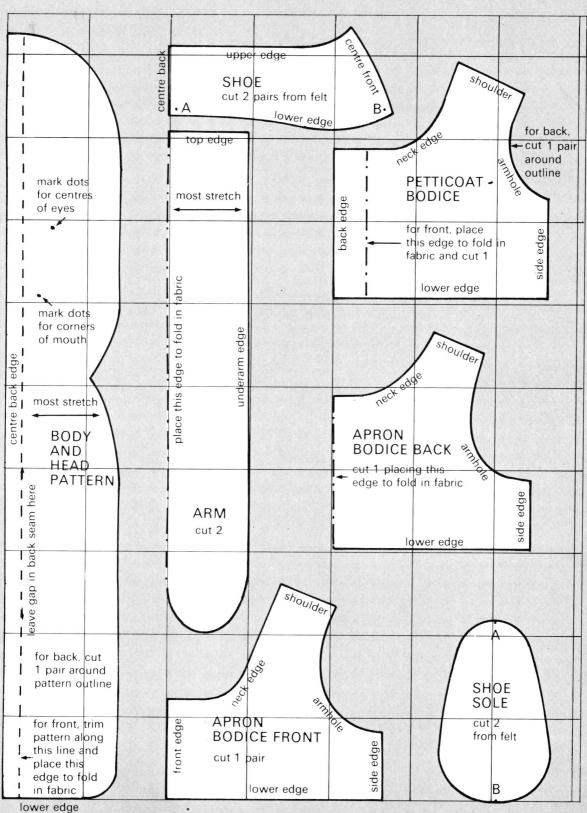

SHOE
cut 2 pairs from felt

centre back

upper edge

lower edge

A

centre front

B

PETTICOAT-BODICE

shoulder

neck edge

armhole

for back,
cut 1 pair
around
outline

back edge

for front, place
this edge to fold in
fabric and cut 1

side edge

lower edge

mark dots
for centres
of eyes

mark dots
for corners
of mouth

centre back edge

most stretch

BODY
AND
HEAD
PATTERN

leave gap in back seam here

for back, cut
1 pair around
pattern outline

for front, trim
pattern along
this line and
place this
edge to fold
in fabric

lower edge

top edge

most stretch

place this edge to fold in fabric

underarm edge

ARM
cut 2

APRON
BODICE BACK

shoulder

neck edge

armhole

cut 1 placing this
edge to fold in fabric

side edge

lower edge

shoulder

neck edge

armhole

APRON
BODICE FRONT

cut 1 pair

front edge

side edge

lower edge

SHOE
SOLE

cut 2
from felt

A

B

each square = 5 cm

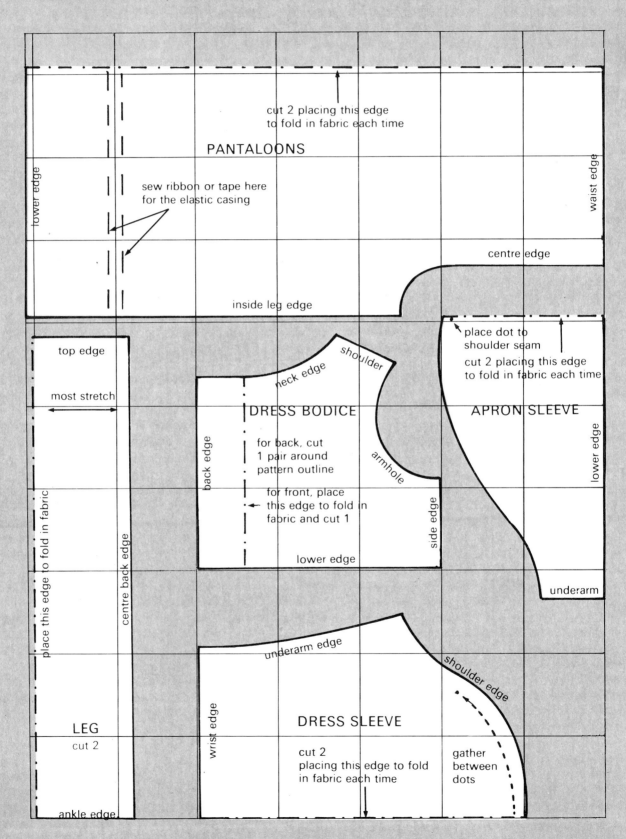

PANTALOONS

cut 2 placing this edge
to fold in fabric each time

lower edge

sew ribbon or tape here
for the elastic casing

inside leg edge

waist edge

centre edge

place dot to
shoulder seam

cut 2 placing this edge
to fold in fabric each time

top edge

most stretch

place this edge to fold in fabric

centre back edge

neck edge

shoulder

DRESS BODICE

for back, cut
1 pair around
pattern outline

for front, place
this edge to fold in
fabric and cut 1

back edge

lower edge

armhole

side edge

APRON SLEEVE

lower edge

underarm

LEG

cut 2

ankle edge

wrist edge

underarm edge

shoulder edge

DRESS SLEEVE

cut 2
placing this edge to fold
in fabric each time

gather
between
dots

Best-dressed Doll

This 43 cm (17 in) rag doll has six different outfits of clothes. All patterns for the doll and clothes are printed full-size for you to trace off the pages.

For the doll you will need: 30 cm ($\frac{3}{8}$ yd) of 91 cm (36 in) wide pink cotton fabric; 250 g ($\frac{1}{2}$ lb) of stuffing; small pieces of white fabric, black and white felt; 20 g ball of 4-ply yarn; red thread and red pencil for facial features; two small buttons for shoes; adhesive.

Important note about the doll patterns on pages 71–3
The body and head is a one-piece pattern but since it is too long to fit on the page, it is printed in two pieces. Trace the body and the head patterns on to thin folded paper, placing folded edge of paper to the dotted lines on patterns when tracing. Mark on all details then cut out patterns with paper still folded. Now open up the patterns and join the head to body at the neckline with sticky tape, to form the complete one-piece pattern.

General notes: Trace all the other patterns off the pages. The doll's legs are straight strips of fabric, and measurements for these are given in the instructions.

The clothes are made in the same basic way using three patterns – bodice, sleeve and pants. Clothes are varied by cutting these patterns to different lengths. When making, read basic instructions, then refer to individual instructions for each garment.

5 mm ($\frac{1}{4}$ in) seams are allowed on all pieces unless otherwise stated. For all hems, turn in raw edges 5 mm ($\frac{1}{4}$ in) then 1 cm ($\frac{3}{8}$ in) and stitch down.

The doll

Legs and shoes: Cut two pairs of shoe uppers from felt. Join them in pairs at fronts then trim seams. For each leg cut a piece of pink fabric 14 by 16 cm ($5\frac{1}{2}$ by $6\frac{1}{4}$ in). For each sock top cut a piece of white fabric 5 by 14 cm (2 by $5\frac{1}{2}$ in). Fold the sock piece, right side out, bringing long edges together. Tack these edges to one 14 cm ($5\frac{1}{2}$ in) edge of

each leg piece, with raw edges level. Now join these edges to upper edges of shoes, with sock tops sandwiched between legs and shoes. Join the remaining long edges of legs and back edges of shoes.

Cut two soles from felt. Keeping legs wrong sides out, oversew edges of soles to lower edges of shoes all round, matching points A and B. Turn legs right side out and stuff firmly to within 2 cm ($\frac{3}{4}$ in) of tops. Tack top edges together, with seams at centre back.

To complete each shoe place a piece of folded white felt over dotted outline on shoe pattern, with fold against front edge then cut out. Sew these pieces to shoe fronts, then sew on buttons as shown in the illustrations on page 67.

Body: Cut two body pieces. Stitch neck darts on each piece and trim folded edges of darts. Join body pieces together round edges, leaving lower edges open. Clip seam at neck. Stitch upper edges of legs to lower edge of one body piece, with right sides facing and raw edges level. Turn body right side out and stuff firmly. Turn in remaining lower edge and slipstitch over seam at tops of legs.

Face: Work mouth in back stitch using red thread, then work back again, oversewing through each stitch. Mark on nose and colour it and cheeks by rubbing with red pencil. Cut eyes from black felt, glue in place then work eyelashes.

Hair: Sew a few loops of yarn to forehead as shown on pattern. For hair at back of head cut about forty 80 cm ($31\frac{1}{2}$ in) lengths of yarn. Backstitch ends of yarn strands to one side of face as shown on pattern. Take strands across back of head and backstitch them to face at opposite side. Repeat this, taking strands backwards and forwards, working up towards top of head until back of head is covered. For a centre parting at back of head, take a long stitch from back of head near neck, to the loops of yarn at front, using matching thread.

For front hair cut about fifty 40 cm (16 in) yarn lengths. Machine stitch through centre of strands and sew this centre parting line to top of head above fringe. Take strands to each side of head, covering ends of yarn that form back hair, and sew yarn strands in place, then plait them and trim the ends evenly.

Arms: Cut two pairs of arm pieces. Join in pairs, leaving upper edges open. Trim seams and turn right side out. Stuff firmly to within 3 cm ($1\frac{1}{4}$ in) of upper edges then stuff lightly. Turn in upper edges and gather them to close. Sew an arm to each side of body, 1·5 cm ($\frac{5}{8}$ in) down from neck.

Her clothes

For all the clothes you will need: Small pieces of fabrics, stretchy fabric for track suit and T-shirt, lace edging, trimmings, narrow elastic, narrow ribbon; small snap fasteners; hooks and eyes; short open-ended zip fastener for track suit; two small buttons. For posy – card, cockleshells, silver bells, fabric flowers and adhesive.

Basic pants: Cut two pants pieces, placing side edge indicated for each garment on pattern to fold in fabric and cutting lower edges as given for each garment. Hem lower edges and if stated thread through elastic to fit legs. Join pieces at centre edges and clip curves. Bring centre seams together and join inside leg edges. Hem waist edge and thread through elastic to fit.

Basic dress: Cut bodice front, one pair of backs and two sleeves as directed on pattern, cutting lower edges as given for each garment. Cut a 2·5 cm (1 in) wide bias strip of fabric long enough to bind neck edge. Join front to backs at shoulders. Turn in and hem centre back edges. Bind neck edge. Hem lower edges of sleeves and thread elastic through to fit arms. Sew trimming to bodice as shown in illustrations. Gather armhole edges of sleeves between dots as shown on pattern and pull up gathers to fit bodice armholes. Sew armholes of sleeves to bodice. Join side and underarm edges.
    Cut dress skirt strip as directed in

individual instructions for each garment. Join short edges taking a 1 cm ($\frac{3}{8}$ in) seam and leaving 6 cm ($2\frac{3}{8}$ in) open at top of seam for back opening. Neaten raw edges of opening and press seam to one side. Hem lower edge of skirt and sew on trimming as shown in illustrations. Gather remaining raw edge of skirt to fit lower edge of bodice and sew in place. Sew snap fasteners to back of bodice.

Underpants: Cut lower edges to line A and trim 1 cm ($\frac{3}{8}$ in) off waist edges. Sew lace trimming to lower edges before threading through the elastic.

Mary, Mary, quite contrary outfit

Pantaloons: Using pants pattern cut lower edges to line B. Sew lace trim to lower hemmed edges. Cut two 16 cm ($6\frac{1}{4}$ in) lengths of elastic and stitch one across each pants leg 3 cm ($1\frac{1}{4}$ in) up from lower edges, stretching elastic to fit as it is being stitched.

Hat: Cut a fabric strip 30 by 50 cm ($11\frac{1}{4}$ by $19\frac{1}{2}$ in). Fold, bringing long edges together and with right sides out, then press. Sew lace trim to folded edge.
    Stitch across hat 3 cm ($1\frac{1}{4}$ in) from fold then stitch again, 1 cm ($\frac{3}{8}$ in) away from first stitching line. Thread elastic through between lines of stitching, to fit head. Join short raw edges. Run a strong gathering thread round through remaining long edges. Pull up gathers as tightly as possible and fasten off. To cover gathered raw edges, gather a circle of fabric round a flat button then sew button on top of gathers.

Dress: Cut lower edges of bodice and sleeves to line A on pattern. For dress skirt cut a fabric strip 16 by 91 cm ($6\frac{1}{4}$ by 36 in).

Apron: Cut a piece of fabric 12 by 16 cm ($4\frac{3}{4}$ by $6\frac{1}{4}$ in). Make narrow hems and sew lace to all but one long edge. Gather this to measure 8 cm (3 in) then bind it with the centre portion of a waistband strip of fabric 5 by 30 cm (2 by $11\frac{3}{4}$ in). Sew two hooks and eyes to ends of waistband.

Posy: Cut a 5 cm (2 in) diameter circle of

card. Glue a frill of lace round edge of card at back. Thread narrow ribbon through bells and glue ends of ribbon to back of card so that bells hang down below posy. Take a length of elastic through card to form a loop at back, knotting ends together at front. Cover front of card with felt and stick on shells and flowers as shown in illustration on page 67.

Nightdress *(not shown in illustrations)*

Using pattern cut lower edges of bodice to line B and make full-size sleeves. Sew trimming to front of bodice before making up. For skirt use a fabric strip 26 by 60 cm ($10\frac{1}{4}$ by $23\frac{1}{2}$ in) and leave 8 cm (3 in) open at top of seam, for back opening.

Blouse and pinafore

Cut lower edges of bodice to line A and cut full-length sleeves.

For bib front join two 6 by 8 cm ($2\frac{3}{8}$ by 3 in) fabric pieces, leaving one long edge open. Turn and press then sew on trimming. Tack raw edges of bib to centre front raw edge of bodice. For straps cut two fabric strips 4 by 17 cm ($1\frac{1}{2}$ by $6\frac{3}{4}$ in). Fold each in half down length, right sides facing, and join long edges and across one short end. Turn and press then tack raw edges of each strap to back bodice, with raw edges level.

For skirt use a fabric strip 14 by 60 cm ($5\frac{1}{2}$ by $23\frac{1}{2}$ in). Sew ends of straps to inside of bib at top then sew on buttons.

Track suit

Note: Take 5 mm ($\frac{1}{4}$ in) seams as usual, but for all hems turn in 1 cm ($\frac{3}{8}$ in) only and stitch down raw edge to prevent fraying.

Pants: Use full-sized pants pattern, then trim 1 cm ($\frac{3}{8}$ in) off waist edges. Sew braid down centre of each pants piece before making up. Put elastic through lower edges.

Jacket: Cut full-sized bodice and sleeve pieces from pattern then trim 1 cm ($\frac{3}{8}$ in) off

underarm edges of sleeves. Note that bodice pieces will be back to front, to make the front zipped fastening.

Sew braid down the centre of each sleeve. Hem lower edge of jacket and thread through elastic. Turn in front edges and sew zip in place, trimming off any excess length of zip at top. Bind neck edges.

T-shirt: (Not shown in illustrations.) Use bodice pattern, cutting lower edges to line C. Make as for basic bodice then bind raw edges of armholes with 2·5 cm (1 in) wide bias strips of fabric.

Jeans and top *(not shown in illustrations)*

Jeans: Use full-size pants pattern and use contrasting thread for all stitching. Make two lines of stitching down centre of each piece. Cut two 5 cm (2 in) squares for back pockets. Turn in top edges and stitch, then turn in remaining edges and lower corners and sew to back of each pants piece before making up. Fake a front 'fly fastening' by working stitching lines on left front before making up.

Smock top: Using pattern cut lower edges of bodice and sleeves to line B. Cut lowered front neckline on bodice front as shown on pattern. Omit elastic at lower edges of sleeves.

For the frill cut a fabric strip 8 by 50 cm (3 by $19\frac{1}{2}$ in). Hem all edges except for one long edge. Gather this and sew it to lower edge of bodice.

Party dress

Using pattern cut lower edges of bodice to line B and sleeves to line A. Cut lowered front neckline on bodice front as on pattern.

For skirt cut a fabric strip 14 by 60 cm ($5\frac{1}{2}$ by $23\frac{1}{2}$ in). Make petticoat as for skirt and sew on lace edging to hang below skirt (*see illustration on page 67*). Catch gathered raw edge of petticoat to gathered raw edge of skirt.

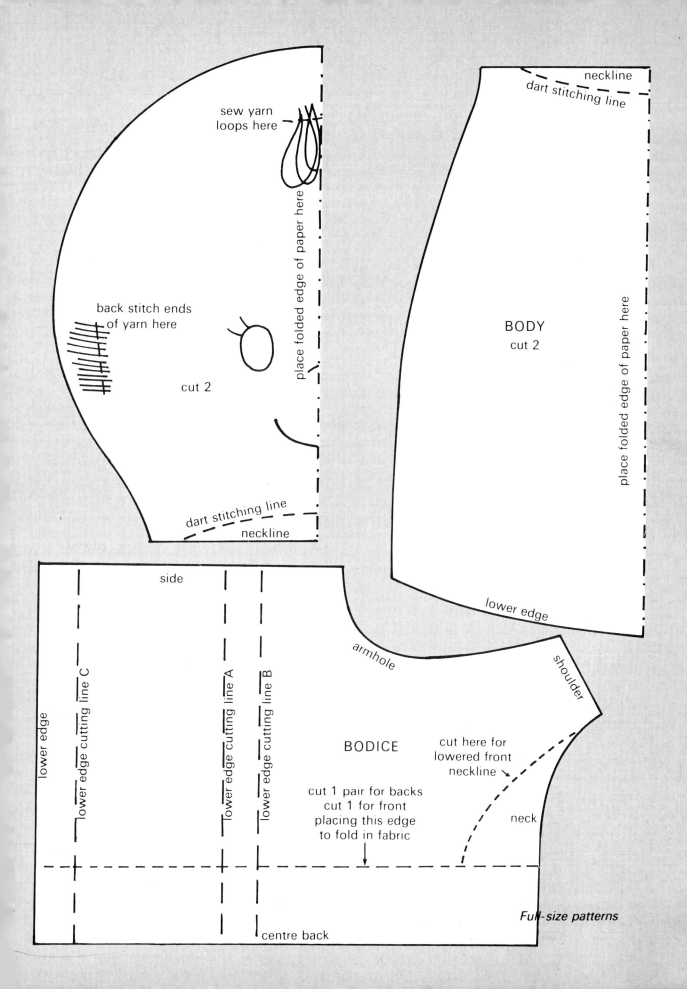

sew yarn loops here

back stitch ends of yarn here

place folded edge of paper here

cut 2

dart stitching line

neckline

neckline

dart stitching line

BODY
cut 2

place folded edge of paper here

lower edge

shoulder

side

armhole

lower edge cutting line C

lower edge cutting line A

lower edge cutting line B

lower edge

BODICE

cut here for lowered front neckline

cut 1 pair for backs
cut 1 for front
placing this edge
to fold in fabric

neck

Full-size patterns

centre back

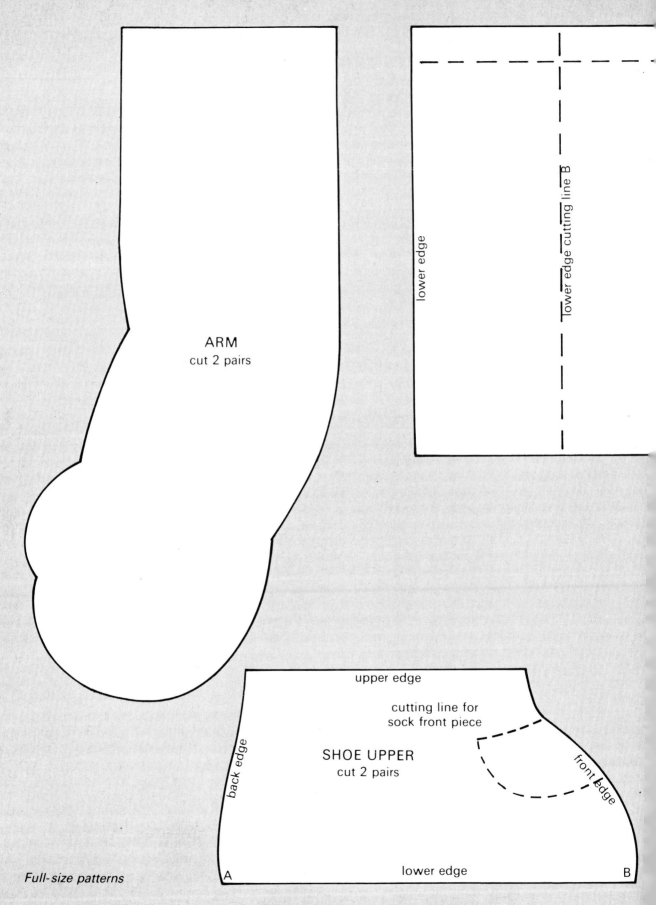

ARM
cut 2 pairs

lower edge

lower edge cutting line B

upper edge

cutting line for
sock front piece

back edge

SHOE UPPER
cut 2 pairs

front edge

A

lower edge

B

Full-size patterns

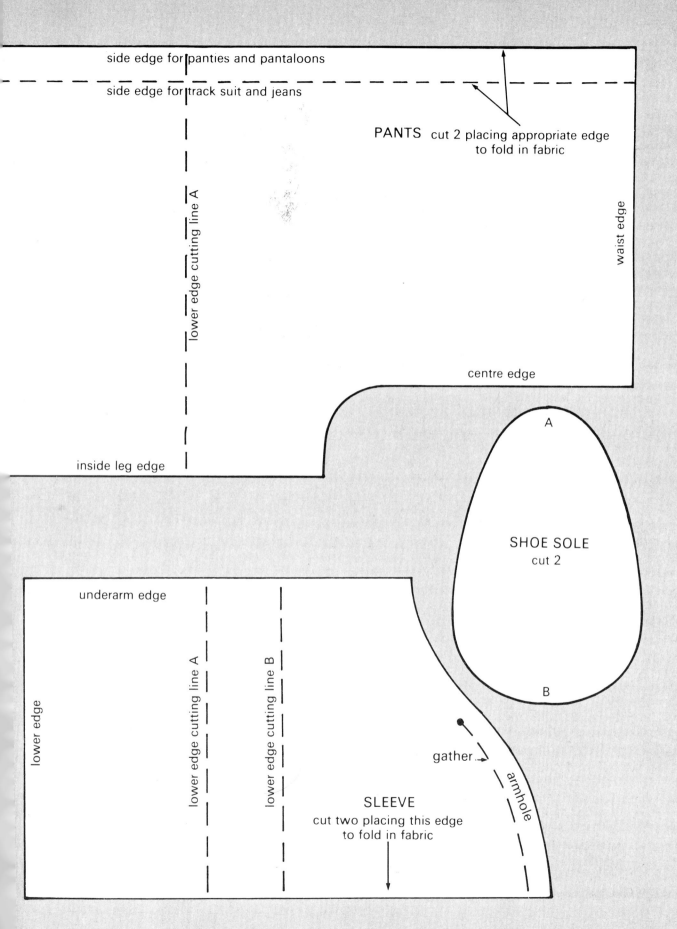

side edge for panties and pantaloons

side edge for track suit and jeans

PANTS cut 2 placing appropriate edge to fold in fabric

lower edge cutting line A

waist edge

centre edge

inside leg edge

A

SHOE SOLE
cut 2

B

underarm edge

lower edge

lower edge cutting line A

lower edge cutting line B

gather

armhole

SLEEVE
cut two placing this edge
to fold in fabric

4
SMALL DOLLS

Baby Bunting Dolls

The cuddliest of baby dolls, about 18 cm (7 in) high, are so easy to sew, complete with their snuggle-down sleeping bags.

You will need: Small oddments of the following – cotton stockinette (or cuttings off a T-shirt or vest); stuffing; printed and plain cotton fabrics; black felt; trimmings; narrow ribbon; thin wadding; shirring elastic; knitting yarn; cuttings off a sock; red pencil; adhesive.

Notes: Trace the body pattern on page 78 off the page on to thin folded paper, placing fold in paper to dotted line shown on pattern. Cut out, then open up to give you a full-sized pattern. Trace hand and bib patterns and cut out.

Take 5 mm ($\frac{1}{4}$ in) seams unless otherwise stated. Join fabrics with right sides facing. When cutting stockinette pieces, make sure that the most stretch in the fabric is going in the directions stated.

The doll

Hands: Cut two pairs of hand pieces from stockinette. Join pairs, leaving wrist edges open. Trim seams, turn right side out and stuff lightly. Gather round hands 1 cm ($\frac{3}{8}$ in) from raw edges, pull up gathers tightly and fasten off.

Head: Cut two pieces of stockinette 6 by 11 cm ($2\frac{3}{8}$ by $4\frac{1}{4}$ in), with most stretch going across the narrow measurement. Join the long edges and trim seams. Gather round one remaining raw edge, pull up gathers tightly and fasten off securely. Turn head right side out and stuff firmly. Run a gathering thread round 2 cm ($\frac{3}{4}$ in) from remaining raw edge, then pull up gathers tightly and fasten off.

Body: Pin body pattern on to two layers of cotton fabric. Trim off fabric level with neck and wrist edges of pattern. Now stitch round close to all remaining edges of pattern. Remove pattern and cut out body 3 mm ($\frac{1}{8}$ in) from seamline, clipping corners and cutting between legs.

Turn body right side out. Turn in wrist edges 1 cm ($\frac{3}{8}$ in) and run round gathering threads. Slip a hand inside each one and pull up gathers tightly round gathers in hand. Fasten off, then sew gathers to hands.

To make thumbs, take a stitch round and through one side of each hand (so that thumbs are pointing upwards); fasten off.

Stuff legs and pin through both layers of fabric across top of each leg. Stuff arms and pin them in the same way. Stuff body lightly then turn in and gather neck edge as for wrists. Insert head and finish as for wrist edges. Remove pins.

For eyes cut two 5 mm ($\frac{1}{4}$ in) diameter circles of black felt (cut these with a leather punch if available) and glue them about halfway down face and 2 cm ($\frac{3}{4}$ in) apart. Mark nose between lower edges of eyes, with red pencil. Make a small smudge with pencil for mouth, 1 cm ($\frac{3}{8}$ in) below nose. Work a stitch with double pink thread across mouth, starting and fastening off thread at top of head. Colour cheeks with pencil.

For ears, take a pinch of fabric at seam at each side of head between levels of mouth and eyes. Sew through the pinch of fabric with small running stitches. Colour ears with pencil.

For hair, split a strand of knitting yarn to make finer strands. Sew a few loops of yarn to top of head, to hang down above eyes.

Cap: Cut a strip of fabric 6 by 23 cm ($2\frac{3}{8}$ by 9 in) to match body. Cut a 3 by 12 cm ($1\frac{1}{4}$ by $4\frac{3}{4}$ in) strip of sock fabric, with most stretch across the long measurement. Fold the sock strip, bringing long edges together. Stitch these raw edges to one long edge of fabric strip with edges level and stretching the sock strip to fit fabric. Join short edges of cap, then gather round remaining raw edge. Pull up gathers tightly then fasten off. Turn right side out. Gather up a 2·5 cm (1 in) diameter circle of sock fabric, putting a little stuffing in the centre, for cap bobble. Sew this to top of cap. Now sew cap to head.

Bib: Pin bib pattern on to two layers of thin cotton fabric. Stitch round close to edge of pattern, leaving a gap in stitching as shown on pattern. Remove pattern and cut out bib as for body. Turn right side out, slipstitch gap. Sew on trimmings and ribbon ties.

The sleeping bag: Cut a 20 by 40 cm (8 by 17½ in) strip of printed cotton fabric for cover, and a strip of plain fabric the same size, for lining. Cut a strip of wadding slightly larger all round than the fabric strips.

Round off the corners of the fabric strips at one short edge. Pin fabric pieces together, right sides facing, with wadding underneath both of them. Join round edges, leaving a gap in short straight edge. Trim wadding level with edges of fabric all round. Turn right side out and slipstitch gap. Sew lace trim to right side of short straight edge.

Now, with lining outside, fold up 15 cm (6 in) at short straight edge of strip to form a pocket (*see diagram 1, below left*). Stitch along each side of pocket, taking 2 cm (¾ in) seams. Using a double strand of shirring elastic in a sewing needle, work small running stitches all round edge of lining in the curved top edge of sleeping bag. Pull up elastic to gather and form the hood, as shown in illustration on page 74–5, then fasten off. Turn the sleeping bag right side out and slipstitch pocket to hood at positions shown in diagram 2 (*below*).

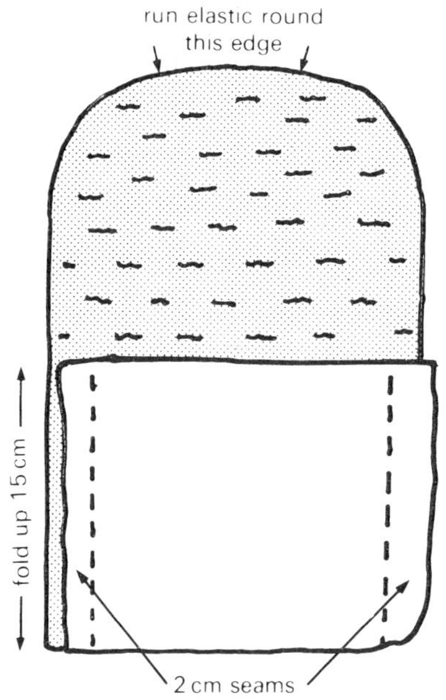

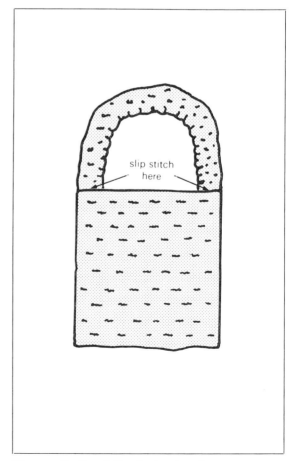

Diagram 1   How to sew up the sleeping bag

Diagram 2   Completing the hood section

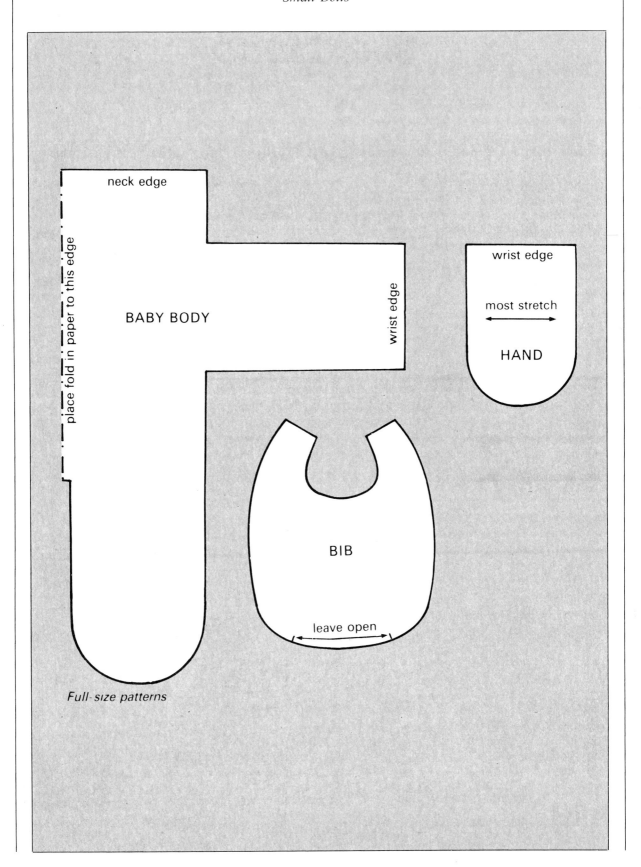

neck edge

place fold in paper to this edge

BABY BODY

wrist edge

wrist edge

most stretch

HAND

BIB

leave open

Full-size patterns

Snowbabies

These little snowbabies, about 15 cm (6 in) tall, can be made as Christmas tree decorations, or as last-minute stocking-fillers for the children.

You will need: Oddments of white fleecy fabric, stuffing, printed fabric, felt, narrow sparkly braid, narrow ribbon, white double knitting yarn, red thread, red pencil, adhesive.

Notes: The pattern outlines are the actual stitching lines. Trace all patterns off the page on to thin paper. When tracing the body pattern, use folded paper and place the fold to the dot-and-dash line as shown; then cut out and open up the folded paper to give you the full-size pattern.

5 mm ($\frac{1}{4}$ in) seams are allowed on clothes.

Basic doll

Pin the pattern to two layers of fleece, with right sides of fabric facing. Machine stitch all round close to the edge of the pattern, leaving a gap in stitching at top of head as shown on the pattern. Mark a pencil line on the fabric, level with edge of pattern at top of head, to denote the seamline. Now remove the pattern and cut out close to seamline all round doll.

Turn doll right side out. Stuff legs and arms, then body and head. Ladderstitch open edges at top of head. Tie doubled sewing thread tightly around neck to shape it.

Cut two 5 mm ($\frac{1}{4}$ in) diameter circles of black felt for eyes (use a leather punch if possible). Glue eyes in place halfway down face, about 1·5 cm ($\frac{5}{8}$ in) apart. When working mouth stitches, take threads through from top of head and fasten off there also. Work a short line for mouth, 1 cm ($\frac{3}{8}$ in) below eyes, using four strands of red sewing thread. Work a tiny vertical stitch at centre of mouth, to pull first stitch into a V-shape.

Sew a few loops of double knitting yarn to forehead above eyes. Mark nose and colour cheeks with moistened tip of red pencil.

Boy snowbaby

Make the basic doll. For pants, cut a 3·5 by 15 cm ($1\frac{3}{8}$ by 6 in) strip of felt. Join ends then put pants on doll, with top edge just under arms. Cut two lengths of braid for braces, one to go over each shoulder. Cross braces over at back and tuck ends inside top of pants. Now sew waist edge of pants to doll, catching ends of braces in as you go. Catch lower edge of pants together at centre front and back, between doll's legs. Glue braid round top edge of pants.

For cap, cut a strip of fabric 5 by 18 cm (2 by 7 in). Join ends of strip. Gather up one remaining raw edge tightly and fasten off. Turn cap right side out. For bobble, cut, gather and stuff a 4 cm ($1\frac{1}{2}$ in) diameter circle of white fleecy fabric. Sew this to top of cap. Put cap on doll as shown in illustration on page 79 and sew the lower edge to head. Glue braid round to cover raw edge.

For scarf, tie a 17 cm ($6\frac{3}{4}$ in) length of ribbon round neck and cut ends at an angle. If the doll is to be hung on the tree, sew a thread loop through top of head and knot the ends.

Girl snowbaby

Make the basic doll. For long hair, cut ten 20 cm (8 in) lengths of yarn and sew centres to top of head. Gather strands to each side of face and sew them there. Tease out ends of yarn and trim them to even lengths. Make hat and scarf as for boy doll.

For skirt, cut a strip of fabric 3·5 by 28 cm ($1\frac{3}{8}$ by 11 in). Join ends then hem one long edge. Gather remaining raw edge and pull it up round doll below arms, then fasten off. Glue braid round waist to cover gathered raw edge.

The hand-held accessories

Christmas tree: Pin the pattern to two layers of green felt and trim felt level with lower edge of pattern. Stitch round, close to remaining edges of pattern. Remove the pattern and cut out tree. Stuff lightly then make trunk as for tree, stitching round pattern pinned to brown felt. Push the trunk inside lower edge of tree and stitch across.

Broom: Cut a 5 by 8 cm (2 by 3¼ in) strip of brown felt. Make 3 cm (1¼ in) long cuts along one short edge, to form the bristles. Roll up the strip across its width and wind sewing thread tightly round handle above the bristles.

Stocking: Make as for tree, using red felt,

trimming felt level with upper edge of pattern before stitching. Glue braid round upper edge.

Parcel: Pin pattern to two layers of felt. Stitch all round, then remove pattern and cut out. Tie braid round parcel.

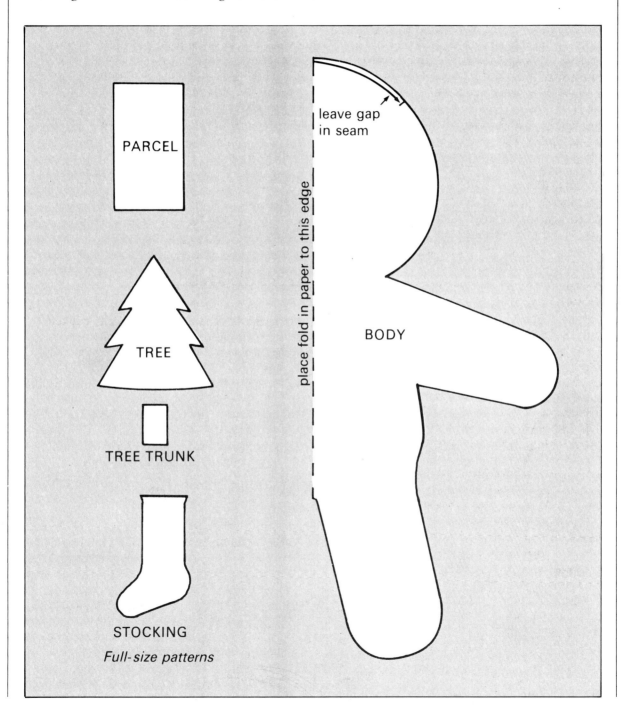

PARCEL

leave gap in seam

place fold in paper to this edge

BODY

TREE

TREE TRUNK

STOCKING

Full-size patterns

5
TOY
HOUSES

Dormouse House

The dormouse (from the French word dormir – *to sleep) can sleep happily through the winter – either underground or in its own snug nest built into a hollow tree, and this family of toy dormice are like their real-life cousins. They are small and furry about 7·5 cm (3 in) high, with bushy tails slightly shorter than their bodies, and they sit up on their hind legs, using their forepaws to hold their food. Their tree house is a touch more fanciful than the usual variety – with two rooms luxuriously furnished down to the last detail. It measures about 33 cm (13 in) across, 18 cm (7 in) high, and it is made in two separate halves hinged together along one wall, with a zip fastener across the roof and down the opposite wall. You can make the complete toy as a soft, squashy dolls' 'house-for-animals' or copy some of the ideas for furnishing an existing dolls' house.*

For the house and furnishings you will need: 1·20 m ($1\frac{3}{8}$ yd) of heavy sew-in Vilene interfacing, 83 cm ($32\frac{1}{2}$ in) wide; 80 cm ($\frac{7}{8}$ yd) of polyester wadding, 91 cm (36 in) wide; for doorbell – a bell (the kind used for birdcage toys, available from pet shops); oddments of fabrics, felt, green fur fabric, double knitting yarn, stuffing, trimmings, braids, lace edging, bias binding, shoe lace and boot lace; a 50 cm zip fastener; dark and light brown permanent marker pens; a pair of tweezers for turning and stuffing very small pieces.

For the dormice you will need: Oddments of fawn fleecy fabric, matching felt, fabrics, trimmings, stuffing; for eyes – six circles of black felt if the toys are for a very young child (or six 3 mm ($\frac{1}{8}$ in) diameter black beads for toys for an older child); brown marker pen; transparent nylon sewing thread for whiskers.

General notes

Suitable fabrics and sewing methods: For the outer house walls (tree bark) use brown tweedy furnishing fabric or coatweight fabric. For the house roof (the cut section of the tree) use smooth fawn fabric. Seams, hems and turnings are 5 mm ($\frac{1}{4}$ in) except where stated otherwise.

Patterns for dormice, easy chair and hearth are given full size on page 90. Trace these off the page on to thin paper. Baby dormouse patterns are given in broken lines, within the dormouse outlines.

Join fabric pieces with right sides facing unless stated otherwise. When sewing items to inside walls of the house, turn the rooms inside out to do this easily.

The stitch-around method: When this is mentioned in instructions, make the item as follows: pin the paper pattern on to layers of fabric stipulated, then stitch around close to the edge of the pattern, leaving a gap for turning. Remove pattern and cut out the item 3 mm ($\frac{1}{8}$ in) from stitching line. Turn right side out and slipstitch gap or proceed as given in the instructions.

The living room

Floor: Make a paper pattern as follows: draw a 36 cm ($14\frac{1}{4}$ in) diameter semi-circle then add 3 cm ($1\frac{1}{4}$ in) to straight edge. Use the pattern to cut two from interfacing, one from wadding and one from fabric suitable for the interior floor of the room.

Place interfacing pieces together, wadding on top and floor fabric right side up on top of wadding. Tack, then sew pieces together round edges. Work stitching lines round the floor to quilt it, parallel to the curved edge, about 2 cm ($\frac{3}{4}$ in) apart. After quilting, the straight edge will have curved inwards slightly. Trim this edge to straighten it. Bind the straight edge with a 4 cm (1½ in) wide straight strip of fabric to match the floor. Press floor.

Walls: Cut a paper pattern measuring 18 by 64 cm (7 by 25¼ in). Cut one pattern shape from bark fabric, one from interfacing and one from wadding. Tack them together round edges, sandwiching wadding between the other two pieces. Turn in bark fabric 2 cm (¾ in) at short edges and stitch this to interfacing. Use pattern to cut a fabric strip for interior walls. Place this on top of interfacing, turn in short edges of fabric strip 3 cm (1¼ in) so that they lie 1 cm (⅜ in) inside the turned-in edges of bark fabric, then sew in place. Tack remaining long edges of strip to interfacing. Now stitch through all thicknesses at long edges, then work vertical lines of stitching up the wall, about 3 cm (1¼ in) apart.

Using the diagram as a guide, cut out door and window openings to sizes given. Bind these edges to neaten them and form door and window frames. Cut two 8 cm (3¼ in) lengths of bias binding for window struts. Fold each in half along length and stitch, then sew turned-in ends of strips to inside of window frame to form four panes.

Sew braid round the outside of the window and the door frames on the outside of the house.

Roof: Cut pieces and stitch as for floor, making the upper piece of fabric the appropriate colour for a cut-section of tree. After trimming straight edge to straighten it, turn it in 1 cm (⅜ in) and slipstitch it in place.

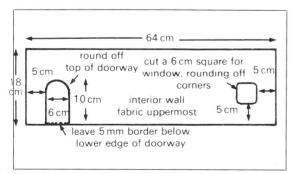

Diagram 1   Showing how to cut window and door openings in the wall

Press roof. Mark a few dark brown lines radiating from centre of roof, then use lighter brown to shade the stitching lines as shown in the illustration on pages 82–3.

Make a skylight window in roof, in same way as for wall window.

To assemble the pieces: Pin, then stitch one long edge of wall around the curved edge of the floor, with interior wall fabric against the floor fabric and raw edges level.

Cut a 6 by 64 cm (2½ by 25¼ in) strip of green fur fabric for grass. Oversew one long edge of the strip to seamline under floor on outside of house, with right side of fur fabric outside.

Cut the remaining long raw edge of fur fabric irregularly, then turn it up loosely on to the wall so that a little fur fabric lies along the ground. Sew the irregular edge to the wall.

Turn room inside out and pin upper edge of wall to curved edge of roof, with outer roof fabric against the tree bark fabric. Sew in place, taking a 1 cm (⅜ in) seam. Turn seam down and oversew raw edges to the inside wall of room. To cover these raw edges, sew the straight edge of lace trim or braid to seamline, then sew fancy edge of the trimming to the wall.

The bedroom: Make exactly as for living room, omitting the door.

To assemble the rooms

Place the rooms side by side, the bedroom on the left, living room on the right, with adjacent walls touching. Oversew these wall edges together securely where they touch, to form a hinge. Open the zip fastener and sew ends of tapes to hinge at top of walls. Pin the zip tapes just inside edges of each room along roof and down the remaining wall edges. Slipstitch edges of roof and walls alongside zip teeth, then oversew remaining outer edges of tapes in place.

Decorating the outside

Doorbell: The bellpull also acts as a tag for holding on to when closing the zip fastener. For a bellpull, cut a 30 cm (12 in) length of shoe lace. Thread this on bell and join lace ends. Make a loop at this end and sew it to top of wall outside the hinge between the rooms.

Window awning: Cut an 11 cm ($4\frac{1}{4}$ in) length of pleated or frilled trimming, neaten ends then sew it above window.

Window box: Cut an 18 cm (7 in) length of 1·5 cm ($\frac{5}{8}$ in) wide braid. Join ends then sew lower edges together. Sew bits of green fur fabric inside box, then sew guipure flowers to fur fabric. Sew sides of box to wall below window.

Mushrooms: Use white stretchy stockinette, such as cuttings off a T-shirt. For a stalk roll up a 3 by 24 cm ($1\frac{1}{4}$ by $9\frac{1}{2}$ in) strip of fabric tightly and sew the end in place.

For mushroom top, gather a 7 cm ($2\frac{3}{4}$ in) diameter circle of fabric, stuff; then push

stalk inside, turning in the gathered raw edges, pull up gathers and sew them to the stalk.

Make various sizes, using smaller strips and circles. Sew stalks to grass and tops to wall where they touch.

Toadstools: Make stalk as for mushrooms. For top, cut a 6 cm ($2\frac{1}{4}$ in) diameter circle of red spotted fabric, and one of stockinette. On stockinette mark 'gills' with a brown pen, radiating from centre. Join the circles round edges, then cut a small hole in centre of stockinette and turn right side out. Stuff, then push in stalk and sew in place. Sew to house as for mushrooms.

Make smaller toadstools as for mushrooms, using a red spotted circle only for each top.

Leaves: Use pinking shears to cut oval leaf shapes from green and brown felt, about 3 by 5 cm ($1\frac{1}{4}$ by 2 in), varying the sizes slightly. Mark on veins, then fold leaves in half and press. Sew brown leaves to grass, green leaves in groups to the bark.

Ladybird: Gather and stuff a 2·5 cm (1 in) diameter circle of red fabric. Hold the ladybird on a needle while marking the centre stripe, spots and face in black pen.

Snail in shell: Cut an 11 cm ($4\frac{1}{4}$ in) length of white boot lace (the broad kind, used for sports shoes). Turn in and gather one end tightly. Stuff, then turn in remaining edge and sew, but do not gather. Rub the boot lace with brown pen then mark a few thin lines along length with darker pen. Grip gathered end with tweezers and roll snail up tightly, pinning then sewing it in place.

Doormat: Sew a piece of towelling outside the door, turning in raw edges.

Chimney: Cut a 7 by 50 cm ($2\frac{1}{4}$ by 20 in) strip of bark fabric. Hem one long edge. Roll strip up tightly and sew in place. Now use sharp scissors to cut rolled-up raw edge at an angle, to fit against the outside wall of house. Sew a bit of wadding in centre top for smoke. Do not sew chimney in place at this stage.

Living room furnishings

Curtain rail and curtains: For the rail, knot ends of a 16 cm ($6\frac{1}{4}$ in) length of brown cord.

For each curtain, hem edges of a 6 by 11 cm ($2\frac{3}{8}$ by $4\frac{1}{4}$ in) piece of fabric, leaving one raw short edge. Turn in this edge a little, then fold it down 1·5 cm ($\frac{5}{8}$ in) and sew it in place. Stitch again 3 mm ($\frac{1}{8}$ in) from fold, then thread curtain rail through. Sew ends and centre of rail to wall above the window.

Door: Cut two 8·5 by 11·5 cm ($3\frac{3}{8}$ by $4\frac{1}{2}$ in) pieces of felt and two of interfacing. Round off one short edge of each piece, for top of door. Work vertical lines of stitching on pairs of felt and interfacing pieces, about 1 cm ($\frac{3}{8}$ in) apart. Join pieces, taking 3 mm ($\frac{1}{8}$ in) seam, leaving a gap for turning. Turn and slipstitch gap, then press.

Mark a 1·5 cm ($\frac{5}{8}$ in) line for letterbox halfway down door, then stitch round line a little away from it. Cut letterbox open, and trim close to stitching.

For flap, cut two oblong pieces of felt to cover letterbox and sew them together round edges, then sew flap above letterbox.

Now sew side of door to inside of doorway, level with inner edge of bias binding. For doorknobs, gather and stuff two 2·5 cm (1 in) diameter circles of felt and sew them to door.

Easy chairs: Pin chair and seat patterns to two layers of fabric. (Note that the seat pattern is the broken line printed within chair outline.) Make chairs using stitch-around method. Stuff lightly, then slipstitch gaps. Oversew lower edge of chair round sides and back of seat.

Make four legs as for doorknobs, and sew them to corners of seat. Sew a bit of lace trimming over back of chair.

Chimney breast, hearth and fire: Pin hearth pattern to two layers of felt and make hearth using stitch-around method. Turn and slipstitch gap. Press, then sew braid round outer edge for fender.

For log fire, roll up short strips of bark fabric and sew ends in place. Sew logs to hearth, with flames of red and yellow fabric, and wadding for smoke.

For chimney breast, cut two 14 by 17 cm ($5\frac{1}{2}$ by $6\frac{3}{4}$ in) strips of red fabric and one of wadding. Mark bricks on one red fabric piece with black pen.

For fireplace opening cut a 5 cm (2 in) wide by 6 cm ($2\frac{3}{8}$ in) high piece out of centre of one short edge of each piece, rounding off top corners. Join pieces round edges, with wadding under fabrics, tapering long edges slightly towards top and leaving top edges open. Trim side seams, and turn right side out. Sew narrow braid round the fireplace opening.

Now sew lower edges of chimney breast to hearth where shown on hearth pattern. Pin the entire assembly against the living room wall, off-centre (*see illustration on endpapers*). Sew side edges in place as pinned, then turn in top edges and sew them to top of wall.

Sew chimney to outside of house, to correspond with position of chimney breast.

Log basket: Join ends of a 12 by 3 cm ($4\frac{3}{4}$ by $1\frac{1}{4}$ in) strip of coarse cotton lace trimming. Sew a 3·5 cm ($1\frac{3}{8}$ in) diameter circle of felt to base. Make logs as for fire.

'Home Sweet Home' sampler: Mark words on a 2·5 by 3 cm (1 by $1\frac{1}{4}$ in) piece of fabric, then sew fancy braid round edge. Sew this to a larger rectangle of felt. Sew sampler to the chimney breast.

Rug: Plait six 2 m ($2\frac{1}{4}$ yd) lengths of knitting yarn to make a 1 m ($1\frac{1}{8}$ yd) length. Coil the plait round edge to edge, sewing it in place as you go. Press.

Toasting fork: Cut a 5 cm (2 in) length of narrow gold gift wrapping braid and knot one end. Sew a 2 cm ($\frac{3}{4}$ in) braid length to the other end, bending it into a curve. Sew fork to chimney breast.

Table: Pin a 7 cm ($2\frac{3}{4}$ in) diameter circle of paper to two layers of fabric (the same as you used for the roof). Stitch all round edge then cut out. Snip a small hole at centre of one piece and turn right side out. Stitch rings round table and colour it as for roof.

For table pedestal, cut a 3 by 40 cm ($1\frac{1}{4}$ by 16 in) strip of bark fabric. Turn in and hem long edges, then roll up the strip tightly and sew end in place. Sew pedestal under table.

Mugs of cocoa, and toast: For each mug roll up a 1 by 7 cm ($\frac{3}{8}$ by $2\frac{3}{4}$ in) strip of felt tightly and sew end in place. Make a thread loop for handle, and buttonhole stitch round the loop. Colour centre of mug brown to look like cocoa.

For plate, cut a 3 cm ($1\frac{1}{4}$ in) diameter circle of felt and sew on a guipure flower for a doyley. For each slice of toast, cut a 1·5 cm ($\frac{5}{8}$ in) square of felt. Colour the edges dark brown, and the surfaces light brown. For melted butter effect, spread the toast with adhesive and leave to dry. Cut toast in triangles.

Shelf and plant: Make the shelf as for table top, using a 6 cm ($2\frac{3}{8}$ in) diameter semi-circle of paper for pattern and leaving a gap in straight edge for turning. Turn right side out. Sew shelf to wall beside fireplace. Use a guipure flower for a lace mat.

For plant pot, cut a 1·5 by 10 cm ($\frac{5}{8}$ by 4 in) strip of felt. Cut a few spiky leaf shapes from green felt and place them at one end of strip. Roll up strip, sew end in place, and also green leaves.

Broom: Fray out one end of an 8 cm (3 in) square of bark fabric. Roll it up tightly and wind sewing thread tightly round and round handle. Bind round top of bristles with contrasting thread.

Bedroom furnishings

Curtains: Make as for living room curtains.

Bed: For base pattern, cut a 12 cm ($4\frac{3}{4}$ in) square of paper rounding off the corners. Pin this to two layers of fabric with one layer of interfacing on top, one layer of wadding underneath. Make bed by stitch-around method. Turn fabric sides out.

Make legs as for doorknobs, using 3 cm ($1\frac{1}{4}$ in) diameter circles of black felt.

For pillow pattern, cut a 4 by 12 cm ($1\frac{1}{2}$ by $4\frac{3}{4}$ in) piece of paper, rounding off corners. Pin this to two layers of fabric, make pillow by stitch-around method and stuff.

Patchwork quilt: Cut twelve 2 cm ($\frac{3}{4}$ in) wide strips of various printed fabrics, 20 cm (8 in) long. Join them at long edges, pressing seams open. Cut this piece across width into eight 2 cm ($\frac{3}{4}$ in) wide strips and join them, reversing alternate strips so that patches are not matched. Cut lining the same size as quilt, join them round edges, leaving gap. Turn and slipstitch gap.

For valance, cut a 3·5 cm ($1\frac{3}{8}$ in) wide strip to go round two short and one long edge of quilt plus 1 cm ($\frac{3}{8}$ in). Hem all except one long edge. Turn in this edge and sew it in place round quilt.

Bed drapes on wall: Hem edges of an 8 by 30 cm (3 by 12 in) strip of fabric. Gather the strip at centre and 5 cm (2 in) from each end. Tie ribbon bows round end gathers. Pin to centre back of wall above bed, then cut a piece of fabric to cover wall within these drapes. Hem edges of this piece and sew it to wall, then sew drapes to wall at gathers.

Bedside shelves: Make these as for the living room shelf.

Candlestick: Roll up and sew a small strip of white felt for candle; sew wick with black thread. Wind and sew a small strip of coloured felt round base of candle.

For candlestick base, stitch round a 2 cm ($\frac{3}{4}$ in) diameter circle of paper pinned to two layers of felt. Cut out and sew base to base of candle.

Family portraits: Use a fine black pen or pencil to trace portraits off page on to thin white fabric. Cut out oval shapes, then sew braid round edges. Sew portraits to wall.

Armchair: Make as for living room chairs. Add patchwork cushion, sewing this as for the bed quilt.

Baby's cot: Make the base as for big bed, using a 5 by 7 cm (2 by $2\frac{3}{4}$ in) paper pattern.

Use a 3 by 5 cm ($1\frac{1}{4}$ by 2 in) pattern for pillow.

For cot sides, use a strip of 4·5 cm ($1\frac{3}{4}$ in) wide coarse cotton lace edging, long enough to go round base plus extra for a seam. Join ends. Sew a 2·5 cm (1 in) wide strip of interfacing round inside of cot to stiffen it, with one long edge, level with base. Cut a slightly wider fabric strip, neaten edges and sew in place to cover the interfacing. Now sew lower edge of cot sides round edge of base. Sew a ribbon bow to one end of the cot.

For valance frill, cut a 4 by 40 cm ($1\frac{1}{2}$ by 16 in) strip of fabric. Join ends and hem long edges, then gather and sew round outside of cot as shown in illustration on endpapers.

For quilt, join two 5 by 6 cm (2 by $2\frac{3}{8}$ in) pieces of fabric. Turn and stuff, then sew a guipure flower to centre.

The dormice

To make mother: Pin body pattern to two layers of fleecy fabric. Trim fabric level with lower edge of pattern. Make mother using stitch-around method. Stuff, then gather lower edge, pulling up tightly and fastening off. Tie thread tightly round neck.

Sew felt circles (or beads) in place for eyes, taking the needle through from one side of head to other, pulling thread tightly to depress eyes into head. Mark nose with pen and work a small stitch for mouth, below nose. For whiskers, use four strands of nylon thread, passing needle through snout. Knot threads each side of snout and trim ends.

Use pattern to cut four ear pieces. Oversew them round edges, leaving straight edges open. Turn, then gather straight edges and sew to head (*see illustration on pages 82–3*).

Cut four foot pieces from fleece and make as for ears. Do not stuff. Sew straight edges under body at front.

For tail, cut a 2·5 by 6 cm (1 by $2\frac{3}{8}$ in) strip of fleece. Oversew long edges together and continue across one short edge, rounding off corner. Turn, then sew open end of tail to back of body.

For dress, join ends of a 5 by 14 cm (2 by

$5\frac{1}{2}$ in) strip of fabric. Hem one long edge and sew on trimming. Turn in remaining raw edge and gather tightly round neck, then fasten off. Add ribbon bow to front.

Cut and make hands as for feet, using hand pattern. For each sleeve cut a 4 by 4·5 cm ($1\frac{1}{2}$ by $1\frac{5}{8}$ in) strip of fabric. Turn in long edges and press. Join remaining raw edges with a gathering thread, pull up slightly and fasten off. Turn sleeves right side out, slip hands in ends and sew in place. Stuff sleeves lightly, then gather top edges and sew sleeves to sides of dormouse, level with neck. Catch sleeves to body at elbows.

To make father: Make dormouse body, ears and facial features as for mother. Make feet and tail, but do not sew them in place.

Make shirt as for mother's dress, using a 4 by 12 cm ($1\frac{1}{2}$ by $4\frac{3}{4}$ in) fabric strip. Make sleeves and hands as before and sew in place.

For trousers, cut two 5 by 7 cm (2 by $2\frac{3}{4}$ in) fabric strips. Join short edges then turn in one remaining raw edge and press. Gather other raw edge tightly and fasten off. Put trousers on mouse and sew top edge to shirt. Now sew feet and tail in place.

Sew narrow ribbon round top edge of trousers for belt, then work a buckle in straight stitches, using sewing thread.

To make baby: Make as for mother except for dress, hands and tail, using the smaller patterns. Make tail as for mother, using a 2 by 5 cm ($\frac{3}{4}$ by 2 in) strip of fleece.

For dress, join ends of a 12 cm ($4\frac{3}{4}$ in) length of lace edging, about 3·5 cm ($1\frac{3}{8}$ in) wide. Gather this round neck as for mother. Make arms as for mother's hands, using baby arm pattern. Sew tops of arms to sides of dress, just below neck.

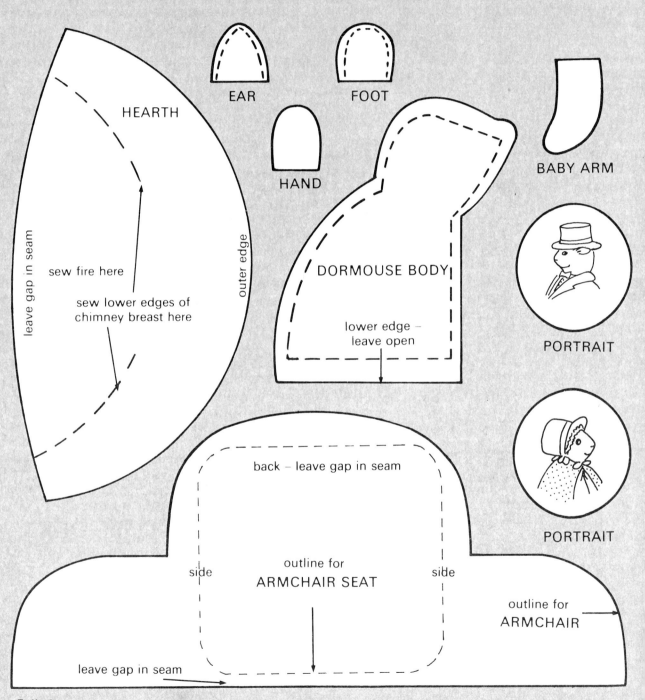

HEARTH

EAR

FOOT

HAND

BABY ARM

leave gap in seam

sew fire here

sew lower edges of
chimney breast here

outer edge

DORMOUSE BODY

lower edge –
leave open

PORTRAIT

PORTRAIT

back – leave gap in seam

side

outline for
ARMCHAIR SEAT

side

outline for
ARMCHAIR

leave gap in seam

Full-size patterns

Dolls' House

No woodworking skill whatever is needed to make this smart bungalow for dolls. It is designed from grocery cartons, with some furniture made of matchboxes (mixed in with bought dolls' house furniture, for added ease).

Smart, modern four-roomed bungalow with garden. Large recep., sunny kitchen/dining room (fully equipped with latest kitchen units), sumptuous bedroom with built-in bed and fitted wardrobes, and luxury bathroom en suite, equipped with vanity unit and shower. Bungalow measures about 70 cm ($27\frac{1}{2}$ in) in diameter, 19 cm ($7\frac{1}{2}$ in) high. Would suit family of dolls roughly 10 cm (4 in) tall.

Notes: All the materials used throughout the house are too numerous to mention in detail here. However, the complete requirements can be ascertained by reading through the instructions for each room.

The four quarters (rooms) of the house are made and joined to each other room by room, as the work progresses.

The house is designed to suit the scale of bought dolls' house furniture and accessories, available from toy shops. The items used here are from the Lunby and 'Caroline's Home' range and, where necessary, bought items are mentioned in the instructions.

You will need: Cardboard grocery box or boxes measuring at least 34 by 34 cm by 18 cm high ($13\frac{1}{2}$ by $13\frac{1}{2}$ in, 7 in high). (Note that a smaller house can be made by drawing out a smaller radius quarter-circle when making the basic rooms.) Small pieces of fabrics and paper for floor- and wall-coverings, and curtains. Small cardboard boxes and cartons such as matchboxes, toothpaste tube and glue tube boxes. Card, paper and Cellophane. Three transparent tops off St Ivel Gold Spread (or transparent acetate film or Fablon). Small mirror tiles and

handbag mirrors. Brass paper fasteners. Cotton reels. Plastic lids of all kinds. Thin wooden dowelling. Discarded plastic sink mat or drainer for garden trellis. For garden plants, small plastic plants as used for aquariums, guipure flowers, green foam sponge. Printed pictures cut from magazines (for pictures, clock faces, etc.). For the kitchen equipment, record player, etc., printed pictures cut from magazines and leaflets from electrical suppliers. Sticky-backed plastic sheeting (such as Fablon) in white and colours and wood effect, for covering furniture. Adhesive. Plasticine. 4·5 m ($4\frac{7}{8}$ yd) of furnishing braid about 1 cm ($\frac{3}{8}$ in) wide.

To make the basic room: Draw out a 34 cm ($13\frac{1}{2}$ in) radius quarter-circle on the glued-down base of the box (*see diagram 1, below*). Now draw lines 18 cm (7 in) up the sides of the box and cut out this shape (see dotted lines on diagram 1). If the box is large enough, another room can be cut from the

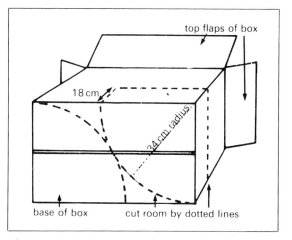

Diagram 1 Cutting a room from a cardboard box. The box shown measures 34 by 58 by 46 cm ($13\frac{1}{2}$ by 23 by 18 in) – large enough to make all four rooms

91

box base as shown in the diagram. If the top flaps of the box are then glued down, two further rooms can be cut from the top end of box if it is more than 36 cm (14 in) high.

Diagram 2 (*below*) shows the room after cutting out. To make a level floor, fill in any missing pieces of card, as shown in diagram. Cover the walls and floor by glueing on fabric or paper, turning and glueing cut edges to wrong side of card. For skirting boards use strips of card 2 cm ($\frac{3}{4}$ in) wide. Note that all items are assembled by glueing unless otherwise stated.

The garden

Cut out basic room. From the centre of the right-hand wall cut out an opening for French windows 12·5 cm wide by 18 cm high (5 by 7 in). Cover right-hand wall. Place transparent lids at back of wall, with tops of lids facing towards garden. Attach sides of lids to back of wall with strips of sticky tape.

Trellis: Cover floor with green fabric or felt. For the trellis which frames the window, cut three strips of sink drainer or mat to fit across top and up sides. Tie strips together with strong thread where they meet. Thread

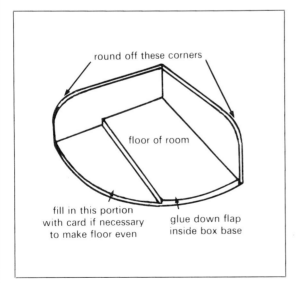

round off these corners

floor of room

fill in this portion with card if necessary to make floor even

glue down flap inside box base

Diagram 2 The shape of each room, after cutting out. Level up floor and trim wall corners as shown

a plastic plant through trellis then place trellis in position. Fix it to the wall with strong thread, taking thread through wall with a needle and knotting it at the back.

Crazy paving: Draw out a semi-circle the width of the window by 12 cm (4$\frac{3}{4}$ in) deep; add to this a 6 cm (2$\frac{3}{8}$ in) square for path and finally a 10 cm (4 in) diameter circle at end of path for fountain. Cut this shape from dark paper. Cut irregular pieces of lighter coloured paper and glue them on for paving. Glue all paved pieces in place and stick bits of foam here and there between the paving stones.

Balustrades: Cut card strips to fit round the curved edge of paving as far as the path – making the strips wide enough to cover ends of Drima thread reels. Mark the card strips to resemble stone then glue the reels between two matching strips as shown in the illustration. Glue the balustrade in place. Cut narrow strips of brown felt for soil on flowerbeds outside the balustrades; glue on foam and guipure flowers.

Urns: For the urns on balustrades use suitable buttons, tying them together through centre holes with thread. Tie in plastic plants too.

Fountain: For lower portion of fountain use a 7 cm (2$\frac{3}{4}$ in) diameter plastic lid off a cheese spread box and on to this glue the push-in centre of sticking plaster dispenser. Glue braid round edge of lid, and blue Cellophane inside lid for water.

For upper part of fountain use the base from a plastic aquarium plant turned upside down. (Alternatively half a table tennis ball could be used.) For the spray of water cut a strip of blue Cellophane 6 by 14 cm (2$\frac{3}{8}$ by 5$\frac{1}{2}$ in) and snip this into strips along one long edge, leaving about 6 cm (2$\frac{3}{8}$ in) un-snipped at other long edge. Roll up strip tightly. Make a hole through upper and lower portions of fountain and join them together by glueing the spray of water through holes.

Kitchen window: On left-hand wall of garden cut opening for kitchen window, making it the size of transparent lid used.

Place the window 6 cm (2$\frac{3}{8}$ in) away from corner of garden and 2·5 cm (1 in) down from top of wall. Cover left-hand wall of garden.

Flowerbed: For wall of flowerbed under the kitchen window cut a 2·5 cm (1 in) wide strip of card the length of the wall. Cut a strip 3 cm (1$\frac{1}{4}$ in) long for end of wall. Mark strips to resemble stones and glue them to garden 3 cm (1$\frac{1}{4}$ in) from kitchen wall.

Fill flowerbed with pieces of chunky cork for soil, glueing them in place. Push plastic plants into cork as shown on page 95.

Garden table and stools: For table use a large cotton reel with a cheese spread lid glued to top. For stools use small lids and golf tees with points cut off (otherwise use Drima thread reels cut in half). Stick centre motifs cut off paper doyleys to tops of table and stools.

Umbrella: Use an umbrella cocktail stick, glueing braid round edge. Otherwise use three paper baking cases flattened out and stuck together, with cocktail stick handle.

The living room

Cut out basic room and place it behind the right-hand garden wall. Mark and cut out rectangle for French window to match the window on garden wall, making the opening slightly larger. Check that the windows will open freely on to the living room.

Cover walls and floor, then glue living room wall to garden wall, holding them together until glue dries with spring clothes pegs or bulldog clips. To fill in the 'threshold' gap between rooms at window, cut a card strip and glue in place. If the windows rub against the floor after carpet is in place, trim lower edges of windows.

Block prints: Cut pictures from magazines and glue them to larger pieces of black card.

Spotlamps: For lighting track, cut strip off edge of a rectangular margarine box. For spotlamps use lids off hair conditioner bottles

or anorak toggles, sewing them to the track. Glue beads inside for bulbs.

Sideboard: Use toothpaste tube box, covering it with wood-effect plastic. For doors cover small pieces of card to match. For handles use halves of self-adhesive spot labels.

Music centre: For record deck use a matchbox tray cut to 1 cm ($\frac{3}{8}$ in) deep. For lid use the transparent lid off a small ring or jewel box. Hinge lid to base with sticky tape. Cover base with wood-effect plastic, then glue on appropriate cuttings for the turntable, etc.

For each stereo speaker cut a matchbox tray in half and slip one half, turned over, inside the other half. Cover to match deck and glue black paper to fronts.

Records and holder: Cut these from magazine advertisement and glue to pieces of card. For record holder use the wire spiral off a small spiral-bound note pad.

Seating units: Each is made up from two matchboxes (or three for the settee unit). Cover each box separately, glueing a 10 cm (4 in) wide fabric strip round it. Snip fabric to corners of box and trim all edges to 5 mm ($\frac{1}{4}$ in) except for one wide edge at each side. Turn in the 5 mm ($\frac{1}{4}$ in) edges and glue down, then glue down remaining portions. Glue covered boxes together as shown in the illustration on page 95, then stick braid round lower edge of each unit.

Coffee table: Use a transparent cheese spread box with braid glued round the sides.

Telephone table: Use lid off hair spray can.

Large plant: Fill a fancy perfume bottle lid with Plasticine and push in dried flowers.

Bookcase: For base use two matchboxes, and two matchbox trays for upper portion. Cover to match sideboard then make and glue on drawer fronts as for sideboard.

Typewriter: Use novelty pencil sharpener.

Row of books: Use magazine cutting glued to a piece of matchbox.

Plant: Fill toothpaste cap with Plasticine and push in a dried plant.

Dog ornament: Use a lucky charm.

Curtains: Use thin wooden dowel for curtain rail with beads glued to ends. Push small screw-in eyes (as used for hanging pictures) into wall to carry the rail. Make curtains to fit, just clear of the floor.

The kitchen

Cut out basic room and place right-hand wall against left-hand wall of garden. Mark on window opening and cut out to match opening in garden wall. Glue walls together as for living room and garden, this time sandwiching the transparent lid between them for window.

Cover walls and floor then glue strip of card in place for window sill. Place bought kitchen sink unit under window.

Floor units and machines: For each cupboard and machine use two matchboxes glued together, standing them on end. Alternatively use one toothpaste or glue box to form several units linked together. Cover cupboards with wood-effect plastic sheet. Cut machine fronts from leaflets or magazine and glue in place. For handles on cupboards cut small oblongs of card and glue to top edge.

Work surfaces: Cut card strips to fit on tops of cupboards and machines, making them slightly wider. Cover with coloured plastic and glue them in place.

Hob unit: Cut hob from a leaflet and glue it to work surface above cupboards.

Double oven: Glue two matchboxes as for base units on to two others. Cover with white plastic and stick on leaflet cutting.

Tall cupboard: Use a suitable small cardboard box. Open it up so it lies flat then cover outside with wood-effect plastic, turning edges to other side of cardboard. Reassemble box, and glue in a card shelf.

Wall units: Cover two matchbox trays to match floor cupboards. Glue a card strip inside each one for a shelf. Link these together with a long shelf over the top then stick a shelf between them.

Extractor hood: Cut matchbox tray 5 mm ($\frac{1}{4}$ in) deep. Cover and glue leaflet cutting to front. Glue hood in place under shelf above hob unit.

Paper towel dispenser: Glue a strip of paper tissue round a thin dowel 2·5 cm (1 in) long. Cut strip of card to fit round dowel. Cover it, then glue all on to wall.

Accessories: For wall clock and posters use magazine cuttings. For chopping board cover card with plastic sheeting.

Dining table and chairs: Cover plastic lid with plastic sheeting then glue it to smaller lid. The chairs were bought.

Curtains: Gather strips of net fabric and glue them to each side of window, tying them back. Glue frill across top of window.

The bathroom

Cut out basic room and cover right-hand wall. For bathroom partition cut a piece of card 14 by 26 cm ($5\frac{1}{2}$ by $10\frac{1}{4}$ in). Round off one top corner, then cut an arched doorway 4 cm ($1\frac{1}{2}$ in) from outer edge, measuring 5 by 12 cm (2 by $4\frac{3}{4}$ in). Glue partition in place, as illustrated. To hold the wall securely glue strips of thin paper at right angles to wall and floor at lower edge. Cover remaining bathroom wall and floor. The shower unit, lavatory and accessories were bought.

Towel ring: Use a plastic ring (from a cracker) or curtain ring, fixing it through the wall with a paper fastener.

Vanity unit: Cover two matchboxes and a matchbox tray with coloured plastic sheeting then stick on contrast pieces for fronts. Make handles as for sideboard. Stand matchboxes on end and glue tray between them at top for drawer. For top surface of unit cut a piece of card 4 by 9·5 cm ($1\frac{1}{2}$ by $3\frac{3}{4}$ in). For basin use a small plastic lid, cutting a hole in unit top just large enough to take the lid, so it fits tightly. Cover the unit top and push lid in place. Stick unit top to unit.

For taps use the clip fittings off clip-on earrings. Bend them to shape then make small slits in top and push fittings in. For mirror back on unit cut a piece of card 8 by 9 cm ($3\frac{1}{8}$ by $3\frac{1}{2}$ in). Cover it to match unit then glue on mirror tiles and posters cut from a magazine. Glue unit and back to bathroom wall. Place small lids and caps on the unit.

Bathroom cabinet: Cover a matchbox tray to match unit, glue on mirror tiles.

Plant: Make as for living room plant.

The bedroom

Cover remaining walls and floor then glue braid round arched edge of doorway.

Door curtain: Fray out a piece of fabric to form a long fringe. Glue it over doorway and stick braid along top edge.

Wardrobes: Use three toothpaste or glue boxes the same size, with a Swan Vestas matchbox for dressing table top. Cover each box with coloured plastic sheeting then for front panels cut pieces of thin card 5 mm ($\frac{1}{4}$ in) smaller all round. Cover card with open-weave fabric to resemble rattan, turning

raw edges to wrong sides of card. Fix paper fasteners through card for knobs then glue panels to boxes.

Stick wardrobes in place in bedroom. Place matchbox between wardrobes, if necessary cutting it to fit. Cover it as for wardrobes.

Glue a handbag mirror to wall between the wardrobes then stick dressing table top in place about 4 cm ($1\frac{1}{2}$ in) up from floor.

Cut a piece of card to go right across tops of wardrobes; cover it to match and glue in place. Place small lids, glass or pearl buttons on dressing table.

Portable TV: Use a plastic novelty toy or a magazine cutting glued to a matchbox.

Stool: Cover a small lid with open-weave fabric and on top of it glue a card circle covered with contrast fabric.

Laundry basket: Cover a lid with fabric as for stool. Make lid of basket from a card circle covered with fabric, with a paper fastener pushed through for knob.

Bed: For raised platform cut a few pieces of card 13 by 16 cm ($5\frac{1}{8}$ by $6\frac{1}{4}$ in). Round off corners at one long edge. Glue card pieces together then cover them with fabric, turning raw edges to other side of card.

For mattress use six matchbox trays glued together (or a complete cardboard box about 11 cm ($4\frac{1}{4}$ in) square by 2 cm ($\frac{3}{4}$ in) deep. Cover mattress with fabric as for base.

For the sheet cut a piece of card 5 mm ($\frac{1}{4}$ in) smaller all round than mattress, cover it with fabric and glue to mattress.

Bedhead: Glue three slide-on matchbox covers together end to end, and cover with fabric to match bed. For headboard cut an arched piece of card the width of bedhead by 12 cm ($4\frac{3}{4}$ in) high. Cover it with open-weave fabric. Cut two 2·5 cm (1 in) wide card strips to fit round curved edge of headboard. Cover one strip with fabric to match headboard and the other to match bed. Glue strips in place. Stick bed to bedhead.

Make lighting track in bedhead as for living room, using small Christmas tree baubles for the spotlamps.

Pillow and quilt: Cut two 4 by 12 cm ($1\frac{1}{2}$ by $4\frac{3}{4}$ in) pieces of fabric for pillow and two 12 cm ($4\frac{3}{4}$ in) squares for quilt. Take narrow seams round edges, turn and stuff lightly then slipstitch gaps.

Books: Cut from magazines and glue to card.

Wall mirror: Use fancy handbag mirror or a small mirror badge.

Baby's bassinet: Stick tops of two matchbox trays together. Cover inside one tray with open-weave fabric then glue trimming round sides of bassinet.

For hood cut a piece of card 1 by 10 cm ($\frac{3}{8}$ by 4 in). Bend it in half and glue ends to sides of bassinet at one end. Glue trimming over this and at end, then make a small pillow and bedcover from trimming.

To complete the dolls' house

Glue final room in place. Cut four quarter-circles of card to fit underneath the rooms. Turn house upside down and glue these card pieces in place, taking care that the quarter-circles join in a different position from the rooms, to strengthen the base.

Glue braid along the top edge of bathroom partition, then across top edges of the rooms and finally right round the outside edges of the floors.

Dolls' house dolls

Parents about 10 cm (4 in) tall; baby about 4·5 cm ($1\frac{3}{4}$ in).

You will need: A pipe cleaner and 1 cm ($\frac{3}{8}$ in) diameter wooden bead for the baby; two 1·5 cm ($\frac{5}{8}$ in) diameter wooden beads and six pipe cleaners for parents; scraps of fabrics, cotton wool, nylon stockings or tights; knitting yarn for hair; marker pens or pencils for facial features; modelling clay or Plasticine for shoes; adhesive. *Note:* Take

3 mm ($\frac{1}{8}$ in) seams on clothes unless otherwise stated.

Baby

Cut a 10 cm (4 in) length of pipe cleaner for body and legs, fold it in half and glue fold into bead. For arms use remaining 6 cm ($2\frac{3}{8}$ in) length of cleaner, tying centre to body pipe cleaner below head with thread. Wrap a tiny bit of cotton wool round body, arms and legs, tying it in place with thread. Bend round 3 mm ($\frac{1}{8}$ in) at ends of pipe cleaners for hands and feet.

Mark on face and hair with pen or pencils then glue a bit of yarn to top of head to cover hole in bead. To cover hands pull scraps of nylon stocking fabric up around hands and tie it round wrists with thread. Trim off excess fabric.

Trace tights pattern on to thin paper and cut out; pin pattern to two layers of stretchy fabric (e.g. cuttings off a sock). Sew round pattern close to edge, leaving top edges open. Remove the pattern and cut out tights. Turn right side out and put tights on baby, glueing waist edge in place. Glue a bit of matching fabric round each arm for sleeves. To cover rest of body cut a strip of ribbon; cut arm slits then glue in place.

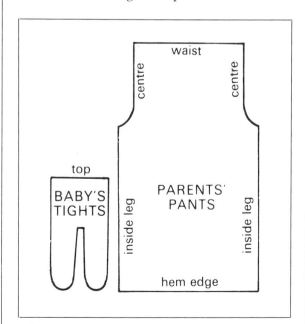

Left Pattern for baby's tights
Right Pattern for parents' pants

Father

Cut two 12 cm ($4\frac{3}{4}$ in) lengths of pipe cleaner for body and legs. Cut a 15 cm (6 in) length of pipe cleaner and fold it in half for arms. Glue the fold and other pipe cleaners into bead.

Wrap cotton wool round body, arms and legs tying it in place with thread. Bend round 1 cm ($\frac{3}{8}$ in) at end of each cleaner for hands and feet. Cover hands as for baby. Model shoes round pipe cleaner feet with clay or Plasticine. Colour clay when dry. Mark on face and hair and glue bits of yarn to head.

Use the pattern to cut two pants pieces from fabric. Turn in hem edges and glue. Join pieces at centre edges, bring these seams together and join inside leg edges. Turn pants right side out. Put them on doll and glue waist edge to waist.

For sweater front and back cut two 3 cm ($1\frac{1}{4}$ in) squares of stretchy fabric. Glue them in place, overlapping and sticking sides under arms and top corners on shoulders. Glue a strip of fabric round each arm for sleeves. Cut narrow strips of fabric, turn in long raw edges and glue down to neaten, then stick these strips round lower edge, wrists and neck edge of sweater.

Mother

Make doll as for father, cutting leg pipe cleaners slightly shorter. Cover head with yarn strands as illustrated. Make pants as for father.

For blouse sleeves cut two 4 cm ($1\frac{1}{2}$ in) squares of fabric. Overlap and glue two opposite edges on each piece. Slip sleeves on arms and sew top edges to body. Gather wrist edges round wrists and glue on trimming.

For body of blouse cut a fabric strip 4 by 10 cm ($1\frac{1}{2}$ by 4 in). Turn in one long edge and glue down then stick on trimming. Place on doll and make small slits at each side so arms can come through. Turn in and glue raw edges of slits. Place blouse on doll again and gather top edges tightly round neck. Glue trimming round neck and tie a narrow ribbon round waist for a belt.

6
PLAY HOUSES

Wendy House

Like every good Wendy house, this design has a smart front door, windows to look out of, and plenty of space inside (about 145 cm (57 in) long, 104 cm (41 in) wide, 135 cm (53 in) tall – to the pitch of the roof). Unlike most Wendy houses, though, this one is made from fabric – and it is constructed like a tent, with pitched roof, end poles and guy ropes.

You will need: For the walls – 4 m (4⅜ yd) of non-woven curtain fabric 172 cm (68 in) wide; for the roof – 1·6 m (1¾ yd) of similar fabric in a contrasting colour; for decorating walls, windows and doors – oddments of non-fray fabrics and felt; net fabric for window glass; fringed braid; narrow white tape; for tent poles – two 152 cm (5 ft) long broom handles, or similar lengths of 2·5 cm (1 in) diameter wooden dowelling; 1 m (1⅛ yd) of strong tape or bootlace for the guy rope loops and tent peg loops; 13 m (14¼ yd) of strong cord or string for guy ropes; twelve tent pegs; black and brown permanent marker pens; adhesive.

Notes: If possible, it is best to use non-fray fabrics (such as non-woven curtain fabric and felt) for all appliqué pieces on the walls. If you are using woven fabrics, allow 1 cm (⅜ in) extra on all raw edges for turnings.

Use dabs of adhesive to hold appliqué pieces in place before sewing them. (Small pieces such as the felt flowers need not be sewn in place if they are stuck down firmly.)

When making up the house take 3 cm (1¼ in) seams on all pieces. Other seams and turnings are stated in the instructions.

The roof

From roof fabric cut two pieces 78 by 150 cm (30¾ by 59 in). Mark a 3 cm (1¼ in) seam allowance along both short edges of each piece. Cut a piece of card to the size and shape shown in diagram 1 (*above right*). Place this card template on one piece of roof fabric, within the seam allowance as shown in diagram 1. Using black marker pen, draw dotted line round V-shape at lower end of

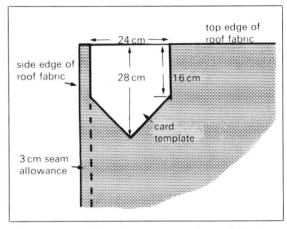

Diagram 1   Marking the pattern on the roof fabric

template. Continue like this, moving template along the roof and drawing round lower edge. Next draw a shallow curved shape (using the edge of a dinner plate) between V-shapes, as shown on the roof illustrated on pages 98–9. Repeat this pattern on the other roof piece. Draw shading below all lines, using a brown marker pen.

The walls

Using the cutting layout shown in diagram 2 (*opposite, top*), cut out the fabric walls to the sizes in diagrams 3 and 4 (*opposite, centre and below*).

To make the front wall (with door and window): Mark on, then cut out, door and window openings to size given in diagram 3. For window and door frames cut 10 cm (4 in) wide strips of fabric to fit sides and lower edges of window, and sides and top of door. Stitch them in place, with inner raw edges level. Turn in all inner raw edges of window

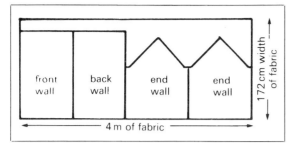

Diagram 2 Cutting layout for the walls

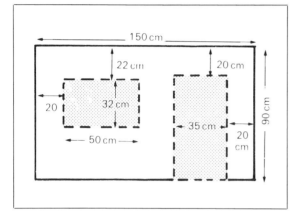

Diagram 3 Front wall, with door and window openings. Cut out back wall the same size, placing window as stated in instructions

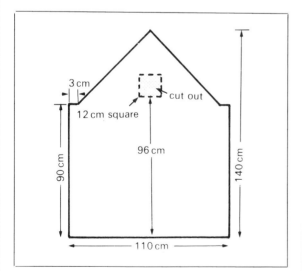

Diagram 4 How to cut out each end wall, with attic window

and door openings 2 cm ($\frac{3}{4}$ in) and press, clipping fabric at corners. Stitch down raw edges.

For mullion window, cut a piece of fabric 40 by 58 cm ($15\frac{3}{4}$ by 23 in). Draw a line all round, 2 cm ($\frac{3}{4}$ in) from raw edges. Mark this

rectangle into six equal 18 cm (7 in) squares. In each square draw round a saucer (about 14 cm ($5\frac{1}{2}$ in) in diameter), centrally placed. Cut out circles. Place window over a piece of net fabric 40 by 58 cm ($15\frac{3}{4}$ by 23 in), to represent glass. Sew pieces together around edges, and around edges of circles. To divide the window into panes, sew on strips of white tape between circles. Now sew window in place behind window opening.

For the striped awning above window, cut a strip of fabric 20 by 75 cm (8 by $29\frac{1}{2}$ in). Sew this centrally above window; sew a strip of fringe to lower edge of awning.

Turn in lower edge of wall 3 cm ($1\frac{1}{4}$ in) and stitch it down. At lower edge of wall under window, sew an irregular strip of green fabric for grass. Cut groups of coloured felt flowers as shown in illustration on pages 98–9 and glue them in place. Sew centre of each flower to the wall.

For the door cut a piece of fabric 58 by 76 cm (23 by 30 in). Turn in all raw edges 2 cm ($\frac{3}{4}$ in) and stitch them down. For letterbox cut a 12 cm ($4\frac{3}{4}$ in) long slit across centre of door, about 28 cm (11 in) up from lower edge. Turn in raw edges of slit 1 cm ($\frac{3}{8}$ in) and stitch, clipping fabric at corners.

For letterbox flap, cut two pieces of fabric 8 by 20 cm (3 by 8 in). Join them round edges, taking a 1 cm ($\frac{3}{8}$ in) seam and leaving a gap for turning. Trim seam, turn right side out and slipstitch gap. Stitch round close to edges then mark on lines with black pen, 1 cm ($\frac{3}{8}$ in) from edges. Sew top of letterbox flap above slit in door. Use black pen to mark door panels on door, making the upper panel about 28 cm (11 in) square and lower panel 28 by 18 cm (11 by 7 in).

For doorknob, cut two 9 cm ($3\frac{1}{2}$ in) diameter fabric circles. Join them round edge, taking a 1 cm ($\frac{3}{8}$ in) seam. Trim seam. Cut a small slit in centre of one piece, turn circle right side out through slit then stuff. Oversew slit and sew knob beside letterbox. Sew top of door in place at back of door frame, with lower edge of door 2 cm ($\frac{3}{4}$ in) above lower edge of wall.

For curtains cut two pieces of fabric 45 by 50 cm ($17\frac{3}{4}$ by $19\frac{1}{2}$ in). Narrowly hem all edges of each piece, except for one short edge. Take 1·5 cm ($\frac{5}{8}$ in) turning twice on this edge. Thread a 70 cm (27½ in) length of tape through these curtain edges and sew tape ends to inside wall above window, keeping it taut. Sew centre of tape to wall.

To make the back wall: Make a window, awning and curtains at centre of back wall, exactly as for window on front wall. Hem lower edge of wall and sew on grassy strip in same way. Sew a green fabric shrub shape to wall each side of window, as shown in illustration on pages 98–9, then glue on flowers as for front wall.

To make the end walls: Cut a small attic window in each wall (see diagram 4). Sew on 8 cm (3 in) wide strips of fabric for window frames and neaten inner edges as for other windows.

For window glass cut a 20 cm (8 in) square of net fabric. Sew white tape across centre to form four small panes. Sew net square to back of window frame. Turn in lower edges of side walls 3 cm (1¼ in) and stitch down, then sew on grassy strips as before.

End wall with birdbox: For the upright post on birdbox cut a strip of fabric 6 by 40 cm (2½ by 15¾ in). For sloping support pieces, cut two strips 4 by 20 cm (1½ by 8 in). For flat table top cut a strip 5 by 32 cm (2 by 12½ in), and slope the sides slightly.

Place them all in position on walls as shown in illustration on pages 98–9, with upright post about 30 cm (11¾ in) away from right-hand edge of wall. Sew all pieces in place.

For birdbox cut a 25 cm (9¾ in) square of fabric. Using illustration as a guide, shape one edge into a pitched roof, and below this taper sides in towards lower edge. Sew paler fabric to front of box and mark on lines, then add a small black felt circle for nesting hole. Sew birdbox on top of bird table.

For climbing nasturtiums, cut leaves of various sizes in different shades of green felt. Mark lines on each leaf with brown pen. Arrange leaves on wall, with the largest leaves at lower edge, and smaller leaves climbing up the wall. Glue leaves in place. Cut red and orange felt flowers and glue them in place.

Cut simple bird shapes in blue and brown felt. Mark on eyes, cut small triangles of black felt for beaks then sew birds to wall.

End wall with hanging sign: For the tub cut a piece of fabric 16 by 24 cm (6¼ by 9½ in). Curve the two short edges to make a tub shape. Stitch on three 3 cm (1¼ in) wide felt strips for the iron bands. Cut a 3 cm (1¼ in) wide strip for trunk of shrub, and green fabric for foliage, as for shrubs on back wall of house. Sew them all to wall, with right-hand edge of tub about 10 cm (4 in) from right-hand edge of wall. Add nasturtiums on grassy strip to left of tub, as for the other end wall.

For house sign, cut a piece of dark fabric 30 by 40 cm (11¾ by 15¾ in). Cut edges to curved shapes. Mark on the lettering of your choice with chalk, then embroider it with yarn.

For the sign bracket cut braid strips – one 52 cm (20½ in) and two 8 cm (3 in) long. Place sign about 20 cm (8 in) from left-hand edge of wall and about 8 cm (3 in) down from edge of window frame. Sew sign in place then sew bracket pieces above the sign.

Joining the pieces

Join roof pieces along top edges, leaving a 4·5 cm (1¾ in) gap at each side of seam, 3 cm (1¼ in) in from each end. (These gaps are for top ends of poles to pass through.) To reinforce the gaps, press seam open then glue small patches of fabric over wrong side of gaps. Turn roof to right side and stitch all round a few times close to edges of gaps. Cut slits in fabric patches to match the gaps.

For guy rope loops cut four 10 cm (4 in) lengths of strong tape or bootlace. Fold each in half to form a loop. Join lower edges of roof pieces to tops of front and back walls, enclosing a guy rope loop in each seam, 3 cm (1¼ in) in from each end. Cut six more 10 cm (4 in) lengths of tape and fold them into loops. Join side edges of end walls to front and back walls, enclosing a loop of tape at hem edge of each seam. Sew a tape loop to each lower corner of doorway.

Join apex portion of end walls to sides of roof pieces, snipping roof seam. Snip off top corners of apex on end walls.

Sharpen 2·5 cm (1 in) at one end of each pole, for driving into the ground. Mark a line round each pole, 10 cm (4 in) from these sharpened ends. Drill a 5 mm ($\frac{1}{4}$ in) diameter hole through each pole, 2·5 cm (1 in) from other end of pole. To support the roof, knot a length of strong cord round and through holes in poles, making the total cord length 144 cm (56$\frac{1}{2}$ in) including thickness of poles.

Now place poles inside house, pushing tops through gaps in roof seam. Using very strong thread, sew roof fabric to poles at these points, working oversewing stitches at each side of gap and taking thread through holes in poles.

For guy ropes at each corner of roof, knot one end of a 170 cm (67 in) cord length through each guy rope loop at roof corner, then knot a loop at other end of cord.

For the guy rope on each pole cut a 210 cm (82$\frac{1}{2}$ in) cord length. Knot one end to fit over the top of the pole; make a loop at other end.

Make a groundsheet from waterproof fabric, to fit the base of the playhouse exactly. Sew a loop of tape to each corner.

To erect the playhouse

The ground should be as level as possible to ensure that the playhouse goes up without creases. Spread the ground sheet out and insert a tent peg at each corner. Now at the centre of each short edge of the ground sheet cut out a 2·5 cm (1 in) radius semi-circle. Push the sharpened ends of the poles into the ground at the centre of these semi-circles and drive the poles in up to the marked lines. Peg out each corner loop of the house and the doorway loops. Peg out the guy ropes coming from the roof corners and then the guy ropes on the poles. Adjust the guy ropes as necessary to achieve a smooth finish.

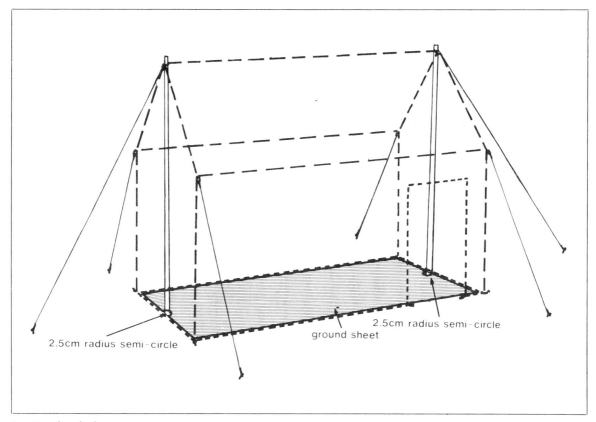

2.5cm radius semi-circle

ground sheet

2.5cm radius semi-circle

Erecting the playhouse

Wigwam

The wigwam measures roughly 1·68 m (5 ft 6 in) high at the peak – and there is plenty of room inside for two or more small braves. It stands on six bamboo canes, and there are fabric loops sewn at the base of the canes to take tent pegs or skewers.
See illustration on frontispiece.

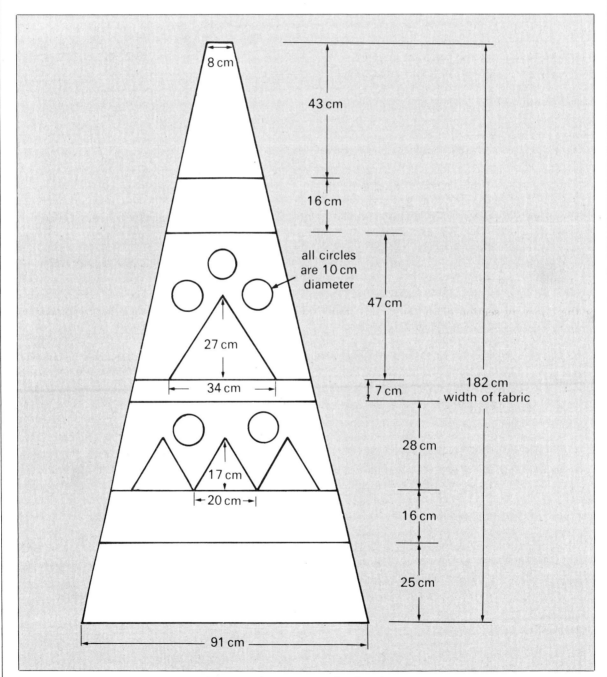

Diagram 1   Pattern pieces for the wigwam

104

You will need: 3·1 m (3⅜ yd) of calico sheeting 182 cm (72 in) wide (or old sheets); six 182 cm (6 ft) long bamboo garden canes; pieces of fabric (or fabric paints) for decorating the wigwam; 3·2 m (3½ yd) of tape about 1·5 cm (⅝ in) wide (or strips of fabric with raw edges turned in).

Notes: If fabric shapes are to be sewn on, use a little glue spread round the edges to stick them in place before sewing.

Add 1 cm (⅜ in) on all raw edges of fabric shapes for turnings, except for the edges which will be taken into the main wigwam seams.

The wigwam

To make: On large sheets of brown paper, or newspaper sheets joined together, draw out the pattern outline to the measurements given in diagram 1 (*opposite*). Then cut out the calico pieces (*see diagram 2, right*), cutting five complete triangles and two half triangles and adding 3 cm (1¼ in) to the straight edges of these as shown (these are for the doorway section of the wigwam). Join the half triangular pieces, taking a 3 cm (1¼ in) seam and leaving 69 cm (27 in) open at the lower edge of the seam for the doorway.

Decorate each section either with fabric pieces or paints, as shown in diagram 1. Turn in and stitch the raw edges of the doorway to neaten.

Sew three 30 cm (11¾ in) lengths of tape or fabric to each of the doorway edges at even intervals, for the ties. Turn in the upper edge of each triangular section 1 cm (⅜ in) and stitch. Hem the lower edge of each section, taking 1 cm (⅜ in) turnings twice.

To assemble: Join two of the triangles at one side, with the right side of the fabric outside and taking a 5 mm (¼ in) seam. Turn wrong side out and stitch again, taking a 2·5 cm (1 in) seam (this forms a casing for the bamboo cane). Stitch securely across the top edge of the seam to close it. Join all the side edges of the triangles in this way to form the complete wigwam.

The finishing touches: For tying the doorflaps back, sew a 30 cm (11¾ in) length of tape or fabric to the edge of each seam inside, on either side of the doorway section, about 52 cm (20½ in) up from the lower edge.

For the loops at the lower edge (to take tent pegs) cut six 12 cm (4¾ in) lengths of tape or fabric. Sew these to the lower edge of the wigwam, placing one beside each seam (*see diagram 3, bottom*). Now slip a bamboo cane inside each seam and oversew across the lower edges of all seams to hold the canes in place.

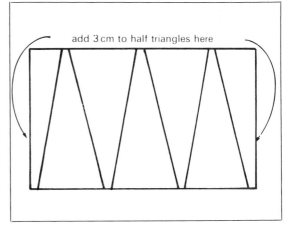

Diagram 2 Cutting out the main pieces from calico

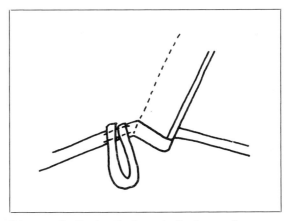

Diagram 3 Sewing the loops to the lower edge

7
NOVELTY TOYS

Sit-upon Elephant

Dumbelle is a giant-sized soft toy elephant (about 43 cm (17 in) high, 67 cm (26½ in) from trunk to back). You can make her from fur fabric and synthetic stuffing so she is washable – and satisfyingly squashy; and she is plenty large enough for toddlers to sit on.

You will need: 1·1 m (1¼ yd) of fur fabric, 138 cm (54 in) wide; 2·25 kg (5 lb) of stuffing; scraps of felt for eyes; oddment of knitting yarn for tail end; oddments of plain and patterned fabric; 1 ball of double knitting yarn for tassels; 1 m (1⅛ yd) of jumbo ric-rac braid; metric graph paper.

To make patterns: Copy the pattern outlines square by square from the diagram. Each square on diagram = 5 cm. After drawing the main body piece, draw the underbody piece separately as marked on the main body pattern. Mark the leg darts on the underbody piece only. Mark all other details on to each pattern piece.

Notes: Follow the cutting-out layout for the placing of patterns on the piece of fur fabric. Take care to reverse the pattern when necessary for cutting a *pair* of pieces. Mark darts and other details on wrong side of each piece. 1 cm (⅜ in) seams are allowed on all pieces unless otherwise stated.

The elephant

Make a small pleat at inner edge of each ear piece as follows. With the right side of ear towards you, fold top dotted line down to meet lower dotted line, making a 1 cm (⅜ in) pleat. Tack pleat in place.

Now join ear pieces in pairs, leaving inner edges open. Trim lower corners, turn right side out, then tack inner edges of each ear together.

On each body piece cut a slit for inserting ear as shown on the body pattern. Slip inner edges of ear between the slit, with raw edges level, then fold body at solid line beyond the slit at each end and tack ear in place. Tack,

then stitch, at position of dotted stitching lines shown on body pattern, thus enclosing ear in stitching.

Join long edges of tail, leaving upper and lower edges open. Turn right side out. Tack upper edges of tail together then sew them to one body piece at position shown on body pattern, with raw edges level.

Now join body pieces together from point A, round trunk and head to point B at back, leaving a gap in seam as shown on pattern. Pull the two layers of fabric apart at end of trunk and stitch dart across end of trunk as shown on pattern.

Stitch the leg darts on each underbody piece. Join underbody pieces to each other at upper edges between points A and B. Now join underbody to body pieces, matching points A and B and leaving lower leg edges open. Sew a foot piece to each lower leg edge, matching the centre front and back points of each foot to the leg seams.

Turn elephant right side out and stuff very firmly in this order: trunk, back legs, front legs and face, then body and head. Ladderstitch gap in seam securely. For tail

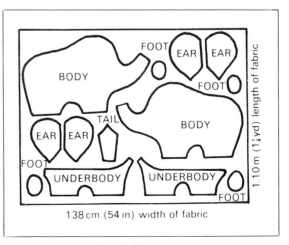

138 cm (54 in) width of fabric

1.10 m (1¼ yd) length of fabric

Cutting-out layout for elephant

end, cut twelve 12 cm (4¾ in) lengths of yarn, and tie a length of yarn round centre. Fold in half at tied position then push the folded ends into end of tail. Gather round end of tail, pull up gathers and oversew securely to hold yarn strands in place. Trim ends evenly.

Cut two eye pieces from white felt, using outline of eye pattern; cut two from blue felt to middle line, and two from black felt to smallest outline. Using white thread, work a highlight on each black pupil, then sew all the eye pieces together. Sew the eyes in place about 6 cm (2⅜ in) apart, with upper edges slightly lower than the height of the end of the trunk.

The saddlecloth

Cut two strips of patterned fabric 18 by 52 cm (7 by 20½ in). For the plain borders, cut four strips of plain fabric 18 by 5 cm (7 by 2 in). Sew ric-rac braid down centre of two plain strips. Join a trimmed plain strip to each short edge of one patterned strip, right sides facing. Sew the remaining plain strips to each end of the other patterned strip, in the same way. Press seams open. Then join complete pieces together round edges, right sides facing leaving a gap in seam for turning. Trim off corners and turn right side out, then slipstitch gap.

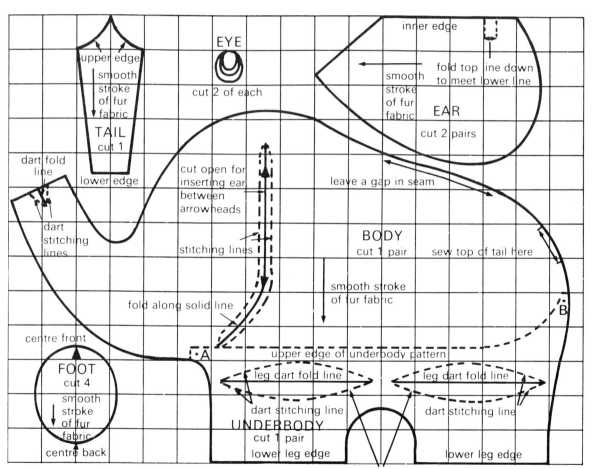

each square = 5 cm

Make twelve tassels as follows. Wind yarn ten times round four fingers. Slip wound yarn off fingers and cut once through the strands. Knot a short length of yarn round centre of strands, then fold at centre and tie another strand of yarn round, about 1·5 cm ($\frac{5}{8}$ in) from top fold. Sew ends of first and second strands down into the tassel. After making all the tassels, slip them on to a thin knitting needle, pushing it through the tops, and steam them over a pan of boiling water to straighten the strands. Trim ends of all tassels to even lengths. Sew six tassels to each short end of saddlecloth, spacing them evenly. Put cloth over elephant's back with ric-rac trimmed borders uppermost, and sew each corner of the cloth to the elephant's body, to hold it securely in place.

The head-dress

Cut two 15 cm (6 in) squares of plain fabric and one 9 cm ($3\frac{1}{2}$ in) square of patterned fabric. Turn in and tack raw edges of patterned square then sew it to centre of one plain square. Join plain squares round edges, right sides facing, leaving a gap for turning. Trim corners then turn right side out and slipstitch gap. Stitch ric-rac round plain border.

Make sixteen tassels in same way as for saddlecloth. Sew one to each corner and three, evenly spaced, along each side. Place head-dress on elephant's head as shown in illustration (*below*) and sew corners to head.

Hickory Dickory Dock (mouse house and clock)

This toy will help the children to learn to tell the time without tears. The clock face is removable, and behind the face is a little mouse house, complete with a family of tiny white mice!

For the clock you will need: A man-size paper handkerchief box measuring about 31 cm long by 16 cm wide by 5 cm deep (12¼ by 6¼ by 2 in); pieces of thin card from cereal packets; scraps of fabric, felt, guipure flowers, ribbon, stuffing, trimmings, braids, thin twigs, medium fuse wire, Plasticine, dried flowers, paper; 2 cm (¾ in) of Velcro Touch and Close Fastener; two metric size Drima reels for weights on clock; two imperial size Drima reels for small tables in house; a Swan Vestas matchbox for the fireplace; small cap off a washing-up liquid bottle and cap off a perfume bottle for plant pots; two small buttons with two holes; 1·2 m (1⅜ yd) of thin cord for pendulum and weights; adhesive; paints or permanent marker pens.

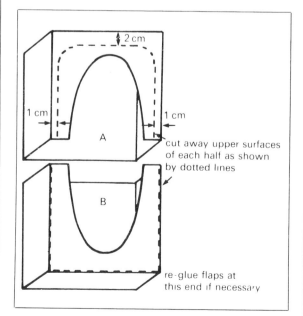

Diagram 1   Cut handkerchief box in half and cut away the upper surfaces

For the mice you will need: Scraps of white fleecy fabric and pink felt; tiny red beads for eyes; scraps of black felt, trimmings, stuffing and white thread; white Velcro Touch and Close Fastener; adhesive.

The clock

For the box at the back of the clock: Cut the paper handkerchief box in half and cut away the upper surface of each half as shown by the dotted lines in diagram 1 (*below left*). Re-glue the end flaps of the half marked B if they are loose. Now slide the half marked A inside the half marked B having first spread the surfaces which will be against each other with glue, to form the box shape shown in diagram 2 (*overleaf*).

Now glue two small loops of narrow ribbon to the top of the box at the back for hanging the clock on the wall (see diagram 2). Reinforce the box on all sides by glueing on pieces of card cut to fit. When glue is dry, pull the ribbon loops to check that they are securely stuck in place. Cover sides and back of box with fabric or felt.

Pierce three small holes in the base of the box as shown in diagram 2 with the pendulum hole 1 cm (⅜ in) from the back and the weights holes 8 cm (3 in) apart. Thread a 40 cm (15¾ in) length of cord through the pendulum hole and knot on the inside of the box then knot the other end. Cut an 80 cm (31½ in) length of cord for the weights, thread one end up through one hole in the box, then across and down through the other hole.

Paint the metric size Drima reels and

111

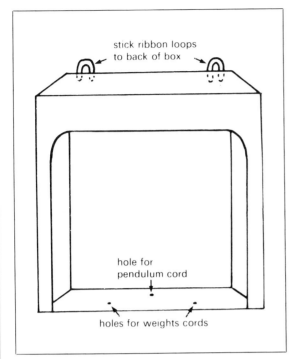

Diagram 2 Pierce holes for the pendulum and weights cords in base of box and attach ribbon hanging loops to the top back

thread one on each end of the weights cord and knot the ends. Sew a 1 cm ($\frac{3}{8}$ in) strip of hooked Velcro around each cord just above the weights.

For the pendulum: Cut two circles of felt 8 cm (3 in) in diameter. Oversew the edges together all round, pushing a little stuffing between them as you go and enclosing the knotted end of the pendulum cord before completing stitching.

To complete: Cover the inside of the box with paper or fabric for the house walls. Make the floor of the house from thin card to fit inside the base of the box and to form a 'bridge' over the cords. Bend the floor to shape as shown in diagram 3 (*below*) making

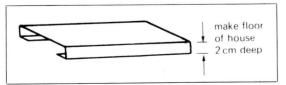

Diagram 3 Make a card floor to fit inside the box base

it 2 cm ($\frac{3}{4}$ in) deep. Cover the floor with paper or fabric and stick it in position in the house. Stick a narrow strip of card round the walls at floor level for the skirting board.

For the fireplace: Use the slide-on cover of the matchbox. Cut off one end so the remainder measures 5 cm (2 in) high. Cut out an arched shape for the fireplace opening measuring 2·5 cm (1 in) wide by 3·5 cm (1$\frac{3}{8}$ in) high. Colour the fireplace black and glue trimming round the arched shape and gold trimming across the lower edge for the front of the grate. Cut a 2 by 5·5 cm ($\frac{3}{4}$ by 2$\frac{1}{4}$ in) strip of card for the mantlepiece, stick it in place then stick trimming round sides and front as illustrated on page 115. Cut a 3 cm (1$\frac{1}{4}$ in) wide strip of card to fit across the fireplace for the hearth, make a tile design on it and stick in place under the fireplace with back edges level. Glue twigs, red paper and cotton wool for smoke inside the grate, then stick fireplace in position. Glue a tiny fabric strip in front of the hearth for a rug.

For the basket of logs: Cut a 2 cm ($\frac{3}{4}$ in) diameter circle of card and glue a strip of narrow braid round it then stick short twigs inside. For the plant pedestal table cut a 2 cm ($\frac{3}{4}$ in) section off one end of an imperial size Drima reel then glue a 2·5 cm (1 in) diameter circle of card to the cut end. Paint the table and stick on lace trimming for a mat. Push a little Plasticine inside the perfume bottle lid then cut small spear-shaped pieces of green paper and push them into Plasticine for leaves. Make the smaller table in a similar way. For the flowering plant, glue dried flowers inside the washing-up liquid cap.

For the gold candlestick: Begin with a 2 cm ($\frac{3}{4}$ in) piece cut off a matchstick. Glue narrow gold braid or cord round and round to cover the match leaving about 5 mm ($\frac{1}{4}$ in) exposed at one end for the candle. Glue a little extra braid round at the base so the candlestick will stand upright. Pare down the candle to make thinner.

For the 'Home Sweet Home' sampler: Cut a 2 by 2·5 cm ($\frac{3}{4}$ by 1 in) piece of card. Glue braid round the edge then mark on words.

Stick narrow strips of card round the edges for the frame.

For the toast on a plate: Cut a 1·5 cm ($\frac{5}{8}$ in) diameter circle of card for the plate and stick on 1 cm ($\frac{3}{8}$ in) squares of light brown felt cut in half. Mark the top slice with darker brown pencil and spread with glue for a 'buttered' effect. For the toasting fork, cut an 8 cm (3 in) length of fuse wire and bend in half. Join in a 4 cm ($1\frac{1}{2}$ in) length of wire and twist all three together for 1 cm ($\frac{3}{8}$ in) then divide wires and bend to make a forked shape. Trim off excess wire and glue on a slice of toast made from felt.

For the clock front: Cut the clock front from card using the pattern shape shown in diagram 4 (*below*), then cut out the arched shape from the centre and discard it. Reinforce the clock front by glueing on one or two more layers of card cut to the same shape. Cover the clock front by sticking on a piece of fabric, cutting it level with the outer edges. Cut away the fabric covering the arched centre opening, leaving enough fabric

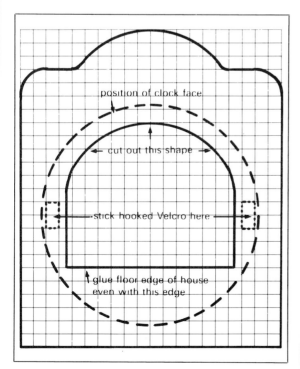

Diagram 4 Pattern for clock front
Each square = 1 cm

for turning and sticking to the other side of the card.

Stick braid round the outer edges of the clock front then stick the clock front in position on the 'mouse house' box so the floor of the house is level with the edge indicated on the clock front pattern.

Stick two 1 cm ($\frac{3}{8}$ in) strips of hooked Velcro to the clock front at the position indicated on the pattern. For the decorative flowers on the clock front cut four 4 cm ($1\frac{1}{2}$ in) diameter circles of fabric for the corners and one 6 cm ($2\frac{3}{8}$ in) diameter circle for the top. Gather round the edge of each circle and pull up the stitches until the raw edges meet then fasten off. Using pinking shears, cut out ten green felt leaf shapes about 3 cm ($1\frac{1}{4}$ in) long. Stick leaves and gathered flowers in place as shown in illustration on page 115, then stick a guipure flower to the centre of each fabric flower.

For the clock face: Cut two 17 cm ($6\frac{3}{4}$ in) diameter circles of yellow felt. Cut an 8 cm (3 in) diameter circle of contrasting felt and sew it to the centre of one large felt circle. Cut a 14 cm ($5\frac{1}{2}$ in) diameter circle of card and stick it centrally between the two larger circles with right sides of the felt outside.

Using black thread, machine the felt circles together, stitching close to the edge, then stitch round again close to the edge of the card. Glue twelve guipure flowers at even five minute intervals round the clock face between the lines of stitching. Cut numbers from black felt or alternatively mark them on the clock face with black marker pen. To make the felt figures, first spread the back of the felt with glue and allow to dry before cutting. Make the number one 5 mm by 2 cm ($\frac{1}{4}$ by $\frac{3}{4}$ in). To keep the other figures in proportion, cut each one from a 1·5 by 2 cm ($\frac{5}{8}$ by $\frac{3}{4}$ in) rectangle of felt. Stick the numbers in place.

Using the pattern shapes given on page 114, cut hour and minute hands from card and stick each of them on to a piece of felt. Cut the felt 3 mm ($\frac{1}{8}$ in) larger all round than the card then stick felt to the other side of the card in the same way. Oversew the edges of felt together all round. To fix the hands to the clock face, pass a double thickness of button thread through both holes of the button then thread all four ends of thread through a needle and take them through the minute hand then the hour hand and then the centre of the clock face to the back. Divide the threads into pairs again and pass through the holes in the second button. Knot thread securely. Sew two 1 cm ($\frac{3}{8}$ in) strips of furry Velcro to back of the clock face at the positions indicated on the clock front pattern.

The mice

Trace off patterns for mouse body, foot, ear and tail pieces given below.

Father mouse: Cut the mouse from fleecy fabric placing the broken line on the pattern to the fold in the fabric. Oversew the raw edges together leaving the lower edge open. Turn right side out and stuff firmly then gather the lower edge up tightly and fasten off. Stick two layers of pink felt together and allow to dry before cutting out the feet. Stick feet in place under the body. Spread both sides of a piece of felt with glue and allow to

dry before cutting out hands. For hands, use the foot pattern trimmed down a little. For arms, cut 1 cm ($\frac{3}{8}$ in) squares of fleecy fabric and glue these around the ends of the hands. Glue arms to body at each side. Cut a tail from felt, spread it with glue and roll up across the width then bend to shape and sew in place. Sew small red beads in place for eyes about 1 cm ($\frac{3}{8}$ in) back from the nose and taking the stitches through the head from side to side. For whiskers, sew strands of white thread through the face and fasten off then trim to length. Cut ears from glued felt and stick to head behind eyes.

For the top hat brim, cut a 1·5 cm ($\frac{5}{8}$ in) diameter circle of felt. For the crown, cut a 1 by 5 cm ($\frac{3}{8}$ by 2 in) strip of felt, spread it with glue and roll up along the length. Glue in position on the mouse's head. Sew a small strip of white furry Velcro to the front of the Father mouse for fixing him on to either of the weights cords.

Mother and Baby: Make in same way. For Mother glue lace to head and toasting fork to one hand. For Baby trim patterns along dotted lines, and reduce feet, hands, arms and ears slightly.

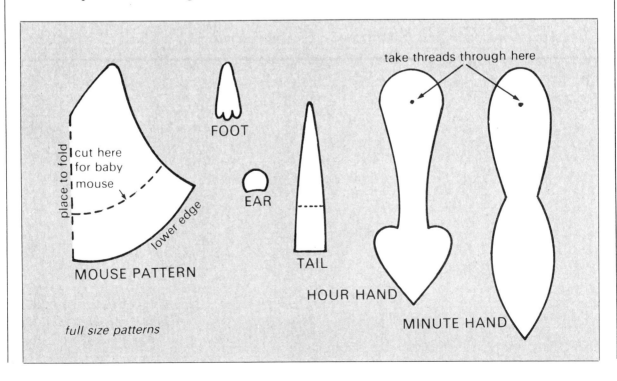

take threads through here

FOOT

place to fold

cut here for baby mouse

lower edge

MOUSE PATTERN

EAR

TAIL

HOUR HAND

MINUTE HAND

full size patterns

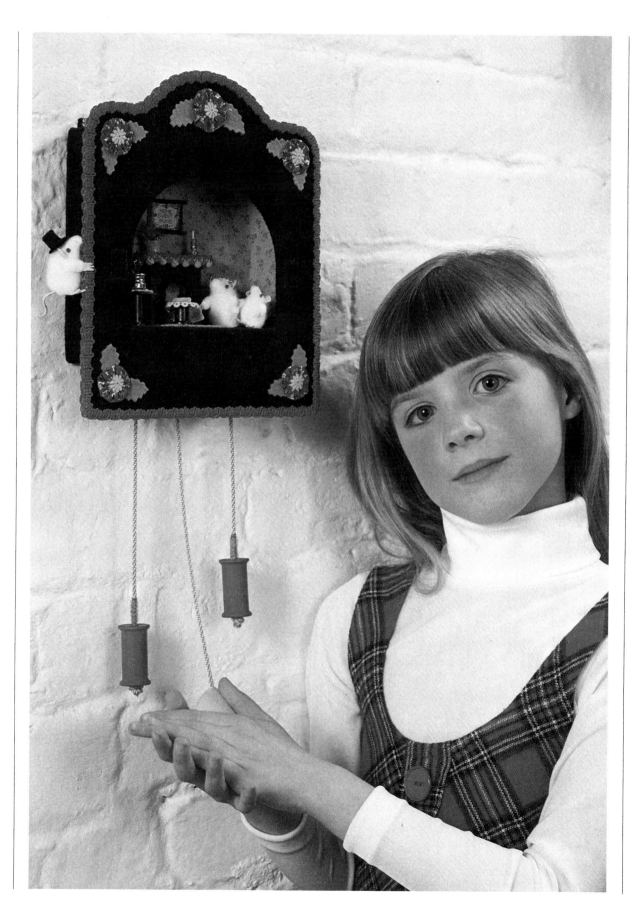

Teaching Teddy

This 35·5 cm (14 in) tall teddy stands securely on a stiffened circular base and she wears clothes that a toddler can learn to take off and put back on. There's how to tie a bow (the bonnet ribbons), fasten a snap fastener (on the knitted shawl), handle hooks and eyes (on the apron), cope with a button and zip fastener (on the skirt), and make that lovely tearing noise with Velcro hook and loop fastener on the underskirt.

You will need: For body and sleeves, 40 cm ($\frac{1}{2}$ yd) of 91 cm (36 in) wide fabric (this amount will make the apron too); 1·2 m ($1\frac{3}{8}$ yd) of 3 cm ($1\frac{1}{4}$ in) wide lace edging; for head and arms, 30 cm ($\frac{3}{8}$ yd) of 138 cm (54 in) wide fur fabric (enough to make two toys); 375 g ($\frac{3}{4}$ lb) of stuffing; strong card for the base (glue several layers of thin card together if necessary); strong thread for gathering; scraps of blue and black felt for facial features; metric graph paper; adhesive.

Notes: Copy patterns off the diagram on page 119 on to graph paper, square by square; each square on diagram = 2 cm. Mark on all details.

Cut out fur fabric pieces with the smooth stroke of fur pile in the direction shown on each pattern piece. 5 mm ($\frac{1}{4}$ in) seams are allowed on fur fabric pieces, and 1 cm ($\frac{3}{8}$ in) seams on all other pieces unless otherwise stated. Join pieces with right sides facing.

The teddy

Body: Cut a 28 by 45 cm (11 by $17\frac{3}{4}$ in) strip of body fabric. Join short edges. For the base cut a 13 cm ($5\frac{1}{8}$ in) diameter circle of card and a 15 cm (6 in) diameter circle of body fabric. Gather round raw edge of fabric circle, place the card circle at centre, pull up gathers tightly and fasten off thread.

Turn in and press one remaining long raw edge of body, then oversew this edge to the fabric round edge of base. Turn body right side out. Stuff body, run a gathering thread round the remaining raw edge, then pull up gathers tightly and fasten off.

Head: Cut a pair of head pieces from fur fabric. Cut the head gusset across the width of fabric, testing the pile of fur fabric for the smoothest stroke before cutting.

Mark mouth lines on wrong side of the head pieces, and also mark centre point of eye on each piece with coloured thread on right side of fabric. Machine stitch along each marked mouth line six times, using black thread, to make a thick line.

Join head pieces at centre front, then insert head gusset between top of head pieces, matching points A. Turn head right side out and stuff firmly, especially at snout. Gather the neck edge of head in same way as for body. Clip the fur pile short above and below the mouth line and around the snout.

Place head on top of body, matching gathers, and hold it in place with darning needles pushed through the head and body fabric. Ladderstitch the head to the body where they touch, working round two or three times to make them secure.

Ears: Cut four ear pieces from fur fabric and oversew them together in pairs, leaving lower edges open. Turn right side out. Oversew lower edges of each ear together, pulling stitches tightly to gather slightly. Sew the ears to sides of head, with inner edges touching gusset seams.

Face: Cut two nose pieces from black felt and glue them together. Sew nose in place at end of snout.

Cut two pupils from black felt and work a highlight on each one in white thread, as shown on pattern. Cut two eyes from blue felt, then stick pupils to eyes. Trim fur pile short around the marked centre points for eyes, then stick eyes securely in place.

116

Arms and sleeves: Cut two pairs of arm pieces from fur fabric. Join them in pairs, leaving upper edges open between dots, as shown on pattern. Turn arms right side out and stuff lower portions, then fill each upper part very lightly. Oversew upper raw edges of each arm together.

For each sleeve, cut a 9 by 20 cm (3½ by 8 in) strip of the same fabric as used for the body. Cut two 30 cm (11¾ in) lengths of lace edging. Turn in one long edge of each sleeve and gather lace edging pieces to fit, then sew in place. Turn in remaining raw edges of sleeves and press.

Slip a sleeve over each arm so that top edge of arm is 5 mm (¼ in) below the top edge of sleeve (see diagram). Now catch the sleeve to arm at the position shown in the diagram, with strong oversewing stitches.

Bring top edges of sleeves together and run a gathering thread along through all sleeve thicknesses. Pull up gathers to measure 3 cm (1¼ in) and fasten off. Gather round lower edges of sleeves at tops of lace edging, pull up to fit arms and fasten off. Sew gathers to arms. Sew the gathered top edges of sleeves securely to each side of the body, 2 cm (¾ in) down from neck.

For neck frill, cut a 60 cm (23½ in) length of lace edging. Join the ends then slip it over Teddy's head. Gather lace up round neck, then pull up gathers tightly and fasten off.

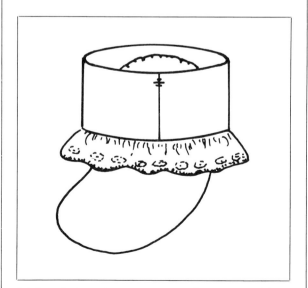

Catch each sleeve to an arm at top of seam, at position of the three small stitches

The clothes

Bonnet

You will need: 30 cm (⅜ yd) of 91 cm (36 in) wide fabric; a small piece of firm Vilene iron-on interfacing; 70 cm (¾ yd) of 2·5 cm (1 in) wide ribbon.

To make: Cut two bonnet brim pieces from fabric and two from interfacing, placing the edge indicated on pattern to a fold each time. Iron interfacing pieces on to fabric pieces. Join brim pieces, taking a 5 mm (¼ in) seam and leaving inner edges open. Trim seam, turn right side out and press. Tack raw edges together. Stitch round, 1 cm (⅜ in) away from outer edge of brim.

For bonnet side piece, cut a 9 by 70 cm (3½ by 27½ in) strip of fabric. Narrowly hem short edges. Gather one long edge to fit inner edge of brim and stitch it in place, taking a 5 mm (¼ in) seam. Trim seam, then bind it with a 2 cm (¾ in) wide bias strip of fabric.

Cut bonnet back piece, placing edge of pattern indicated to fold in fabric. Narrowly hem lower edge. Gather the remaining raw edge of bonnet side piece to fit curved edge of bonnet back piece, and stitch in place. Trim and neaten this seam.

Cut ribbon in two pieces and sew one to each side of bonnet on outside, just behind the brim, forming the end of ribbon into a small loop.

Petticoat

You will need: 30 cm (⅜ yd) of 91 cm (36 in) wide fabric; 1 m (1 yd) of lace edging; a small piece of Velcro hook and loop fastener.

To make: For the skirt, cut a 20 by 91 cm (8 by 36 in) strip of fabric. Fold over one long edge 5 cm (2 in) and press. Stitch along, 5 mm (¼ in) away from fold to make the first tuck. Make another tuck in the same way, 2 cm (¾ in) above first. Narrowly hem long edge nearest to tucks and sew on lace edging. Join short edges of skirt strip from hem edge, leaving 7 cm (2¾ in) open at top of seam. Press seam open and neaten raw edges of opening. Gather waist edge of petticoat to fit around Teddy.

For waistband, cut a 5 by 48 cm (2 by 19 in) strip of fabric. Bind the gathered edge of skirt with waistband strip, taking 5 mm ($\frac{1}{4}$ in) seams and letting the excess length of waistband extend at one end of skirt opening, for overlapped fastening. Sew Velcro to this overlap.

Skirt

You will need: 30 cm ($\frac{3}{8}$ yd) of 91 cm (36 in) wide fabric; 1 m (1 yd) of ric-rac braid; a 2 cm ($\frac{3}{4}$ in) diameter button; a 10 cm (4 in) zip fastener.

To make: For the skirt, cut a strip of fabric 18 by 91 cm (7 by 36 in). Cut waistband as for petticoat. Stitch ric-rac along skirt strip,

2 cm ($\frac{3}{4}$ in) away from one long edge, which will be the hem edge of skirt. Join short edges of skirt from hem, leaving 10·5 cm ($4\frac{1}{4}$ in) open at top of seam for zip fastener. Insert zip into open edges.

Narrowly hem lower edge, then gather waist edge and attach waistband as for petticoat. Make a buttonhole in the extended end of waistband and sew button to other end, to correspond.

Apron

You will need: Fabric left over from making body; 1 m (1 yd) of narrow braid; two large hooks and eyes.

To make: For apron, cut a piece of fabric 12 by 18 cm ($4\frac{3}{4}$ by 7 in). Round off corners at one long edge. Narrowly hem edges, except

for long straight edge. Sew braid round the hemmed edges. Gather raw edge to measure 10 cm (4 in).

For waistband, cut a strip of fabric 6 by 48 cm (2½ by 19 in). Turn in all raw edges 5 mm (¼ in) and press. Fold the waistband in half down length and stitch edges together, inserting gathered edge of apron at centre of waistband. Sew hooks and eyes to ends.

Shawl

You will need: A small ball of 4-ply yarn; a pair of No. 5 (5½ mm) knitting needles; one large snap fastener.

To make: Cast on 90 stitches. Work in garter stitch (every row knit), decreasing 1 stitch at each end of every row until 2 stitches remain. Knit these 2 together then fasten off. Sew snap fastener halves to points.

Shopping bag

You will need: Scraps of fabric, iron-on interfacing and trimming.
To make: Cut two 10 cm (4 in) squares of fabric and two of interfacing. Iron interfacing pieces on to fabric pieces. Join the squares, taking a 5 mm (¼ in) seam and leaving one edge open.

Keeping the wrong side out, open up and flatten seams, then at each lower corner, bring side and lower seams together and stitch across at right angles to seams, 1·5 cm (⅝ in) away from corners. Trim off corners. Turn in remaining raw edge 1 cm (⅜ in) twice, and stitch in place. Turn the bag right side out and sew on trimming as shown.

For the handle, cut a strip of fabric 4 by 18 cm (1½ by 7 in). Turn in all raw edges 1 cm (⅜ in) and press. Bring long edges together, then stitch all round strip. Sew the ends of the handle to the top of the bag at sides, inside the top edge.

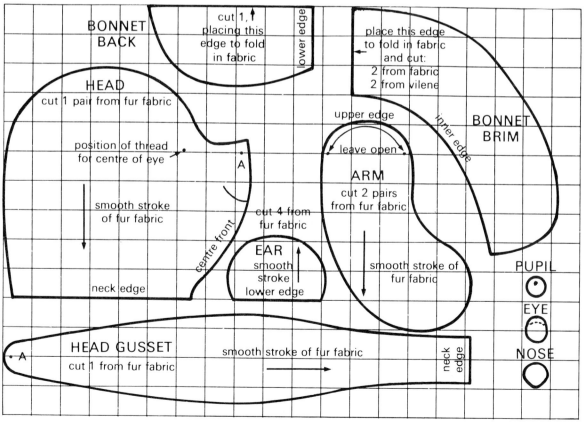

Each square = 2 cm

Punch and Judy Booth

A great favourite with children for generations past, Punch and Judy still pull the crowds at the seaside, at fairs and fetes throughout the year.
This Punch and Judy booth is designed for children to operate. It stands about 165 cm (5 ft 5 in) high, 84 cm (2 ft 9 in) wide, and 61 cm (2 ft) deep. It is fairly easy to make from fabric, and slotted into the corners are wooden poles, pared down at one end so they can be driven into the ground. The flag-decked guy ropes can be pegged out taut to keep the booth upright.
Six glove puppets complete the show.

The booth

You will need: Four 180 cm (6 ft) lengths of 2·5 cm (1 in) diameter wooden dowelling, for the corner posts; 3·4 m (3¾ yd) of 138 cm (54 in) wide striped ticking or other fabric, for the booth; 40 cm (½ yd) of 91 cm (36 in) wide fabric for decorating sides and top of stage; 70 cm (¾ yd) of 91 cm (36 in) wide fabric for the frill at lower edge of stage; 2·3 m (2½ yd) of 91 cm (36 in) wide plain fabric for top and back flap of booth; 1·6 m (1¾ yd) of fringe; 3 m (3¼ yd) of giant ric-rac braid; 9 m (9⅞ yd) of strong string or cord for the guy ropes; oddments of fabrics for the flags; four tent pegs; 20 cm (¼ yd) of Velcro touch and close fastener.

Making the booth

For the front cut a piece of fabric 170 cm long by 88 cm wide (67 by 34½ in). Cut the remaining 170 cm (67 in) length of fabric in half down its length for the side pieces of the booth. Hem top and bottom edges of all pieces, taking 2·5 cm (1 in) turnings twice.

Turn in 5·5 cm (2¼ in) on each long edge of front piece and press. *Note:* These creases mark the eventual seam lines when the booth pieces are assembled. All decorative pieces round the stage should be sewn on within these lines.

To make the stage opening on the booth front, pencil mark the outline (see solid line on diagram 1 (*right*)); draw another rectangle 5 cm (2 in) inside the first one then cut this

out. Snip to the corners of large rectangle then turn fabric to *right* side of booth and press along marked lines. Turn in raw edges 2·5 cm (1 in) and stitch down all round rectangle.

For the sides of stage cut two fabric strips 19 by 38 cm (7½ by 15 in). Turn in long edges 2 cm (¾ in) and tack. Sew these pieces in position (*see diagram 1, below*), keeping them within the crease lines and overlapping the stage opening about 5 mm (¼ in).

For the top of stage cut a fabric strip 18 by 79 cm (7 by 31 in). Trim one long edge to a curved shape (*see diagram 2, opposite top left*). Now cut another piece in the same way

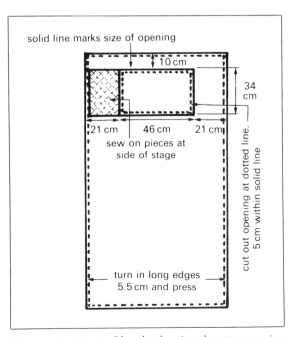

Diagram 1 Front of booth, showing the stage opening

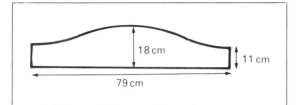

Diagram 2 Shaping for the pelmet at top of stage opening

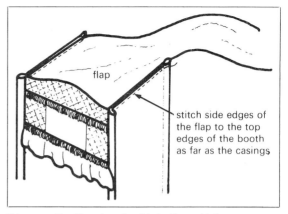

Diagram 3 Showing the fabric flap which covers top and back of booth

for lining (using ticking left over from the booth front). Join top pieces round edges, taking 1 cm ($\frac{3}{8}$ in) seam and leaving the long straight edges open. Trim seams, turn right side out and press. Sew on ric-rac trimming as shown in illustration on page 122.

Pin the top piece in place on booth front, with raw edges level with top edge of stage. Sew in place, taking stitching all round edges of top piece including the top curve. Slipstitch back of curved piece to top edge of booth front. Sew on fringe to cover lower raw edges.

For the frill cut fabric into two 35 by 91 cm ($13\frac{3}{4}$ by 36 in) strips. Join them at one short edge. Take narrow hems on side edges and a 2·5 cm (1 in) turning twice on one long edge. Sew ric-rac to this edge. Gather remaining raw edge to fit across the booth below the stage; sew in place. Sew on fringe to cover gathered raw edge.

Assembling the booth

With right sides facing, join each side of booth front to one long edge of each side piece, taking 1 cm ($\frac{3}{8}$ in) seam. Turn seams to bring wrong sides together and stitch again, 4·5 cm ($1\frac{3}{4}$ in) away from first seam line. This forms casings for the wooden poles at the two front corners (*diagram 3, above right*).

Turn in remaining long edges on the booth side pieces 1 cm, then 4·5 cm ($\frac{3}{8}$ then $1\frac{3}{4}$ in). Stitch in place to form casings for the two remaining poles (see diagram 3).

For the flap which goes over the top and back of the booth, cut a 224 cm ($88\frac{1}{4}$ in) length of plain fabric, 84 cm (33 in) wide. Make 1 cm ($\frac{3}{8}$ in) turnings twice on all edges. Slipstitch one short edge to the top front edge of booth behind the stage pelmet. Machine the sides of strip to the top edges of

the booth sides as far as the casings for poles (see diagram 3). This forms the roof of the booth and the rest of the fabric hangs down the back as a loose flap.

Round off one end of each wooden pole for the top ends and pare the other ends to blunt points for driving into the ground. Bore a 5 mm ($\frac{1}{4}$ in) diameter hole through each pole, 5 cm (2 in) down from the top. Slip a pole into each casing, with the holes just showing above fabric. Using strong thread, sew fabric to poles through holes.

For each guy rope cut a 2 m ($2\frac{1}{4}$ yd) cord length. Tie one end through hole in pole, loop other end to take tent peg. For flags cut small fabric triangles. Narrowly hem edges then sew flags to cords.

Setting up the booth

Keep all corners square and the fabric taut when driving the poles into the ground. Drive in each pole a bit at a time until the fabric touches the ground, then peg out the guy ropes. Now tie another piece of cord across the back through the holes in tops of poles to provide a support for the back flap. To hold the flap in place, sew Velcro strips at intervals to the flap and booth.

The puppets

You will need: Pink felt for hands and heads of Punch, Judy and policeman, crocodile's mouth and baby; white felt for Joey's head and hands; green felt for crocodile; pieces of felt or fabric for bodies; scraps of felt, fur fabric, knitting yarn, trimmings, ric-rac braid; iron-on Vilene, ribbon and pieces of nylon stocking or tights; 1 m (1⅛ yd) of fringe for Joey's hair; four bobbles or beads for Punch; a 12 cm (4¾ in) length of 1 cm (⅜ in) diameter dowelling for Punch's stick; two beads for crocodile eyes; four small and one larger silvery button for policeman; thin card for

neck and hand tubes; black marker pen; red pencil for colouring faces; stuffing; adhesive; metric graph paper; tracing paper.

Notes: Using the diagram on page 125, draw out all pattern pieces square by square on to metric graph paper, following directions given on diagram. Join all pieces with right sides facing, taking 5 mm ($\frac{1}{4}$ in) seams unless otherwise stated. For an adult puppeteer, the body patterns may need to be enlarged.

Punch

For the head: Cut front and back head pieces from pink felt. Join front pieces at face edges and back pieces at centre back edges, trim seams. Join front and back round sides leaving neck edges open and a gap in the seam at the top of the head. Trim seams and turn head right side out. Cut a 7 by 20 cm ($2\frac{3}{4}$ by 8 in) strip of thin card for the neck tube, roll it up along the length to make a tube to fit the index finger (about 2 cm ($\frac{3}{4}$ in) in diameter for an older child, larger for an adult. Secure the end of the card with sticky tape then cover one end of the tube with sticky tape to seal it. Push the sealed end into the head so the neck edge of the head is level with the open end of the tube. Stick the neck edge of felt to the tube, easing felt to fit. Stuff the head firmly through hole in top of head, working evenly round the tube and pushing small pieces of stuffing very firmly into the nose and chin. Ladderstitch opening at top of head.

Colour nose, cheeks and chin with moistened red pencil then work colour into felt by gently rubbing with a wet piece of cloth. Cut out eye pieces and a narrow strip of red felt for mouth. Glue in place.

Cut one pair of hat pieces from red felt then join them leaving lower edges open. Trim seam, turn right side out and stuff the point. Sew hat to head as shown in illustration (*opposite*), pushing in more stuffing to make a firm shape. For hair, cut a 2 by 16 cm ($\frac{3}{4}$ by $6\frac{1}{4}$ in) strip of black fur fabric. Stick it round back of head, level with lower edge of hat. Stick trimming round

lower edge of the hat and then stitch a bobble or bead to point.

Cut ears from two layers of pink felt stuck together. Sew one to each side of the head just inside short edges of fur fabric.

For the body: Cut two body pieces from red felt and join them at side and shoulder edges. Clip into seam allowances at curves and turn right side out. Turn in neck edge 1 cm ($\frac{3}{8}$ in) and push neck edge of head inside it. Slipstitch neck edge of body to head. Cut one pair of hump pieces from red felt and join them leaving the straight edges open. Trim seam, turn, stuff, then sew to centre back of body about 3 cm ($1\frac{1}{4}$ in) down from neck edge.

For the hands: Cut two pairs of hand pieces and join them round the edges leaving wrist edges open. Trim seams and turn right side out. For hand tubes, cut two 3 by 12 cm ($1\frac{1}{4}$ by $4\frac{3}{4}$ in) strips of thin card. Roll up to fit inside hands then secure card and seal ends of tubes as for neck tube. Stuff ends of hands and thumbs then slip sealed ends of tubes inside hands, stick wrist edges to other ends of tubes.

Push hands 1 cm ($\frac{3}{8}$ in) inside wrist edges of body so thumbs are pointing upwards, sew in place. Stick trimming round wrists to match hat.

Cut a 36 cm ($14\frac{1}{4}$ in) length of 4 cm ($1\frac{1}{2}$ in) wide ribbon and gather along one edge. Join the short ends, pull up gathers then sew round neck for ruff. Sew bobbles or beads down front of body. Round off one end of dowel for Punch's stick.

Judy

Make head as for Punch except for hair and ears. For hair, sew the centre of a small hank of black yarn measuring 18 cm (7 in) across, to centre of forehead. Sew looped ends to head at each side.

For mob cap: Cut two 24 cm ($9\frac{1}{2}$ in) diameter circles of fabric. Join them round edges, leaving a gap for turning. Trim seam, turn right side out then slipstitch gap. Gather round cap 2·5 cm (1 in) from edge, pull up gathers to fit on head then fasten off. Stuff cap lightly then sew to head. Sew ribbon bow to top.

Make body and hands as for Punch but if using woven fabric, add 5 mm ($\frac{1}{4}$ in) to wrist edges and 1 cm ($\frac{3}{8}$ in) to lower edges for hems. Make hems before sewing to hands. Stick trimmings round wrists. For shawl, cut a 17 cm ($6\frac{3}{4}$ in) square of fabric and fray out the edges, fold diagonally and place round neck. Stitch to secure at centre front and back of body.

Policeman

Make head in the same way as for Punch but using the policeman's front head pattern. For nose, cut out a 2·5 cm (1 in) circle of pink felt, gather round the edge then stuff the circle firmly as you draw up the gathers. Sew nose in place about 6 cm ($2\frac{3}{8}$ in) up from neck. Cut moustache from brown felt and stick under nose. Cut a 3 by 16 cm ($1\frac{1}{4}$ by $6\frac{1}{4}$ in) strip of felt for hair and stick in place. Make ears as for Punch and sew in place. Cut eye pieces from felt and glue in place.

For chin strap on helmet, stick a strip of narrow ribbon under chin, up sides of face to top of hair as illustrated on page 122. Cut two helmet pieces from blue felt then join them leaving lower edges open. Trim seam, turn right side out then stuff top and place on head. Sew to head at top of hair line at position indicated by dotted line on the pattern, adding more stuffing if necessary. Stick narrow ribbon round sewing line. Sew large button to front of helmet.

Make body and hands as for Punch using blue felt for body. Stick a 1 cm ($\frac{3}{8}$ in) wide strip of blue felt around neck, then sew on buttons down front of body.

Joey the clown

Make head in the same way as for the policeman using white felt. Make the hands from white felt. Make nose as for the policeman but use a 3 cm ($1\frac{1}{4}$ in) diameter circle of red felt. Sew in place. Cut out eye and mouth pieces from felt and glue in place. For hair, sew strips of fringe to head from side to side placing the first strip level with nose. Sew fringe to top of head working outwards in a spiral.

Make body as for Punch if using felt or as for Judy if using fabric. Sew ribbon bow to neck at front.

For sausages: Cut a 4 by 22 cm ($1\frac{5}{8}$ by $8\frac{5}{8}$ in) strip of double thickness nylon stocking or tights fabric. Fold the strip down its length and join long edges. Gather up one end tightly then turn right side out. Stuff about 5 cm (2 in) of the casing for each sausage, tying thread round before stuffing the next one.

The baby

Cut two baby pieces from pink felt. Join them leaving a gap at the lower edge. Trim seam and turn right side out. Stuff, then ladderstitch the gap. Tie a strand of thread round neck then colour cheeks with moistened red pencil and work facial features with small stitches. Stick a bit of trimming to chest below neck. Cut a 20 cm (8 in) square of fabric for shawl and fray out the edges. Fold diagonally and wrap round baby. Make small stitches here and there to hold shawl in place.

Crocodile

Cut two crocodile body pieces from green felt. Trim a little off one piece at mouth end as shown by curved broken line on pattern, for lower jaw. Join pieces along sides from points A to B. Cut one gusset piece from pink felt using head portion of body pattern and placing the fold in the felt to the dotted line shown on the pattern. Trim off one end of gusset at broken line to correspond with lower jaw. Stick white ric-rac braid round edge of gusset so one wavy edge is level with the edge of the felt. Now stick or iron on a piece of Vilene interfacing to other side of gusset piece for reinforcing. Sew gusset in place at open end of body so ric-rac trimmed side of gusset is against the body pieces. Trim seam and turn crocodile right side out. Cut a piece of thin card in the same way as the gusset piece then trim 1 cm ($\frac{3}{8}$ in) off the outer edge all round. Place folded cardboard

piece inside mouth then open up mouth and sew the card to felt at the fold with a few stitches. Sew on beads for eyes and glue on tiny ovals of felt for nostrils as shown on the illustration on page 14.

Cut two pairs of leg pieces from green felt. Join them in pairs leaving a gap at the top edge. Trim seams, turn and stuff, then ladderstitch gaps. Sew a leg to each side of the body where indicated on pattern (*below*).

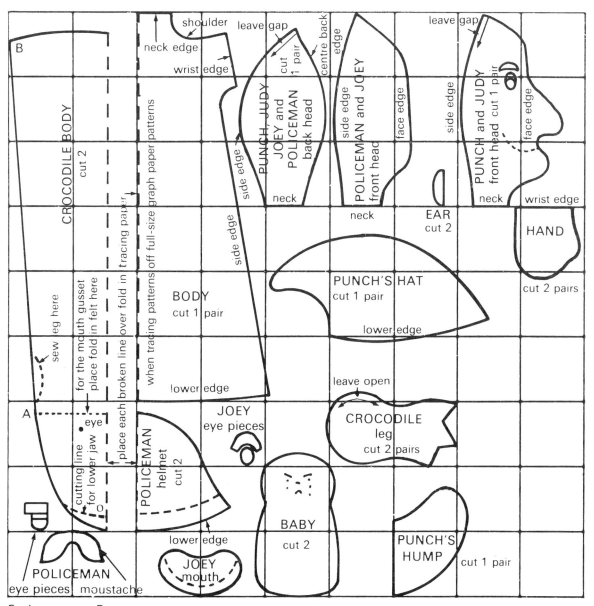

Each square = 5 cm

Nursery Rug

Here is a play rug in the form of a village scene. It is complete with removable toy houses, trees, train and little people.

The playtime rug measures 1 m by 122 cm (39½ by 48 in). You will need three pieces of fabric of this size to make the basic rug. Old cotton sheeting can be used for two layers, and a piece of old blanket for the third (to add body to the rug). Oddments of fabric can be used for the fields, road and river pieces.

You will need: 3 m (3¼ yd) of 122 cm (48 in) wide fabric for the basic rug (see left); oddments of fabric – brown and green for fields, blue for river, grey for road, brown for walls beside road, and stuffing for shaping these walls; 50 cm (⅝ yd) of 122 cm (48 in) wide striped fabric for railway and

8 m ($8\frac{3}{4}$ yd) of tape about 1·5 cm ($\frac{5}{8}$ in) wide for railway lines; 60 cm ($\frac{3}{4}$ yd) of 138 cm (54 in) wide green fur fabric for binding edges of rug and for hedges.

Notes: Seams and turnings are 1 cm ($\frac{3}{8}$ in) unless otherwise stated. When sewing fabric pieces to rug, leave all edges raw – these will be covered by fur fabric hedges.

Rug

To make: Take one piece of fabric for the basic rug. Using pen or pencil, mark lines on fabric for river and roadway, using the measurements shown on diagram 1 on page 128 as a rough guide. Trace drawn outline of river off the rug and cut blue fabric river. For road cut a 12 cm ($4\frac{3}{4}$ in) wide grey strip.

Keeping fabrics flat, tack raw edges of road to rug at positions marked, then sew as tacked. Tack and sew river in place in the same way. Machine stitch wavy lines along river, using blue and white thread. (If you have some net scraps cut these into wavy pieces and sew them along river.)

For railway, first cut two 100 by 12 cm ($39\frac{1}{2}$ by $4\frac{3}{4}$ in) strips of striped fabric. Sew these along short edges of rug, with raw edges of railway and rug level. Next cut two 12 cm ($4\frac{3}{4}$ in) wide strips to fit long edges of rug and sew them in place, turning in short ends of strips to mitre corners (*see diagram 1 on page 128*). Sew on tape for railway lines, spacing them 2 cm ($\frac{3}{4}$ in) apart and placed centrally on striped fabric, and angling them round corners.

Now cover remainder of rug by stitching on green and brown fabric pieces for fields – the main shapes can be traced off the rug and then divided into smaller fields if desired, to suit the fabrics available. Sew a small piece of fabric in centre of river for an island, as shown in the illustration opposite.

Place the rug on top of the two other basic rug pieces, right side up. Tack, then stitch them all together round raw edges. Keeping rug flat, tack then machine all layers together along edges of road, river and round inner edge of railway.

Cut four 8 cm (3 in) wide strips of fur fabric for binding round edges of rug. Sew to right side of rug first, then turn and oversew remaining raw edge to wrong side.

For hedges, cut 4 cm ($1\frac{1}{2}$ in) wide strips of fur fabric; trim strips a little narrower at intervals for an irregular effect. Sew on these strips by hand to cover raw edges of fields, river and railway as follows: Backstitch one raw edge of hedge strip over raw edge of fabric on rug (*see diagram 2 on page 128*), with right sides of fabrics facing. Turn in remaining long raw edge of hedge strip and slipstitch it over raw edge of adjacent piece of rug fabric.

For stone walls alongside road, cut 8 cm (3 in) wide strips of fabric and sew in place as for hedges, enclosing a little stuffing; turn in and sew ends of walls.

The toys

You will need: Scraps of fabrics, felt, trimmings, stuffing; toilet roll tubes; 'Smarties' tubes; Plasticine; small empty cardboard boxes; thin strong card; adhesive.

Notes: When directions state 'Reinforce cardboard', this means sticking on extra layers of card cut to fit sides, base, etc., to strengthen. 'Cover with fabric' means sticking on fabric.

Hill

Use seven toilet roll tubes, cut to 8 cm (3 in) long. Stand them on end, with one in the centre and others grouped round it. Bind round them with sticky tape to hold them together. Stuff all tubes with paper. Glue a piece of card on top of tubes. Glue a larger piece of card to base.

To cover the hill cut a circle of fabric about 36 cm (14 in) in diameter and stick top of hill centrally to wrong side of the circle. Snip round edges of circle, spread round edges on wrong side with glue and stick these to card underneath the hill, creasing fabric to fit. Make a path by sewing a strip of brown fabric from top to base of hill. Sew on 'bushes' of green fabric.

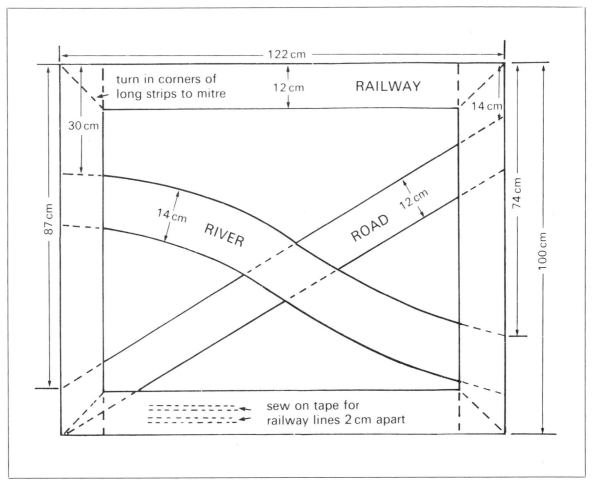

Diagram 1   Showing layout of the play rug

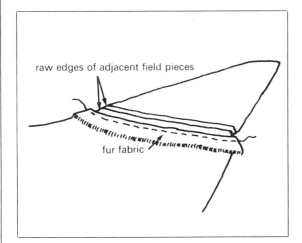

Diagram 2   Sewing hedge strip over raw edge of field

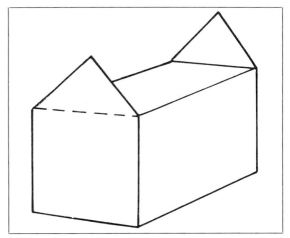

Diagram 3   End walls of house, cut from card with triangular tops for pitch of roof

Ruined tower

Cut a strip of strong card 16 by 26 cm ($6\frac{1}{4}$ by $10\frac{1}{4}$ in). Cut one long edge in a wavy line for the ruined top of tower. Cut out an arched doorway and a small window. Cover both sides of card with fabric cut a little larger all round than card. Overlap short edges; oversew fabric edges.

Road bridge over river

Cut three 9 by 20 cm ($3\frac{1}{2}$ by 8 in) strips of card. Bend each into an arched shape to fit over river, then stick them all together. Cut a 9 by 22 cm ($3\frac{1}{2}$ by $8\frac{1}{4}$ in) strip of grey fabric to match road, and two 6 by 20 cm ($2\frac{3}{4}$ by 8 in) strips of wall fabric. Sew one long edge of each wall strip to one long edge of grey strip (as if to bind edges); stick grey strip to bridge, turning short ends of grey fabric under bridge and sticking them down. Turn raw edges of wall strips under bridge and stick down, enclosing a little stuffing. Oversew raw ends of walls to neaten, then stab stitch along each wall, pulling stitches tight to make it stand upright.

Pond

Cover an irregular 10 cm (4 in) diameter circle of card with blue fabric; stitch as for river and stick green fur fabric round the edge.

Houses

The large house shown is based on a Brillo soap pads box; the smaller house uses a Vileda sponge/scouring pad box.

Stuff the box with paper and glue down end flaps or openings. Cut end walls from –card, incorporating a triangle at top for pitch of roof (*see diagram 3, opposite*). Stick end walls in place; cover walls with fabric.

Cut roof from card, folding it to fit over top of house and making it slightly larger all round. Cut another card roof the same size, glue both together then cover roof with fabric and glue on top of house.

Cut doors and windows from felt and stick in place as shown in illustrations. Glue bits of fur fabric round house for grass.

Train

For the engine cut a strip of felt 10 by 15·5 cm (4 by 6 in). Oversew short edges together to form a tube.

Cut two felt end pieces from pattern. Oversew one end piece to one end of tube, placing seam in tube in position shown on pattern. From card cut two end pieces a little smaller than pattern. Place one inside engine against sewn-on end piece. Cut a card piece 4·5 by 9·5 cm ($1\frac{3}{4}$ by $3\frac{3}{4}$ in) for base and place it inside engine, then stuff firmly. Stick remaining end card piece to remaining felt end piece then sew in place at open end of engine.

For chimney use a cork or tapered plastic lid. Cover it with felt and glue in a bit of cotton wool for smoke. Cut a small hole in top of engine, insert chimney, then sew felt on chimney to engine.

For back wheels cut two 4 cm ($1\frac{1}{2}$ in) diameter felt circles; for front wheels cut two 3 cm ($1\frac{1}{4}$ in) diameter felt circles. Stick them to sides of engine. Stick on narrow braid to trim, as shown in illustration on page 131.

Make waggon from a small cardboard box (the one shown contained a toothpaste tube; the carton was cut to half length and the top was removed). Reinforce box, cover with felt, inside and out, then glue on 2 cm ($\frac{3}{4}$ in) diameter circles of felt for wheels. Attach waggon to engine with tape.

Church

Use a macaroni or cereals box, cut to make it shorter. Make as for houses, with a steeper pitched roof.

For the belfry you need a small bell. Cut a strip of card and bend it to fit round bell, allowing enough space for bell to move inside the shape. Cover card with fabric, sew bell to top so it hangs down inside the shape then glue belfry to roof.

Station

Use a shallow box lid, and stick on strips of card for end walls and roof. Reinforce card and cover with fabric.

Trees

Cut a 5 cm (2 in) section off closed end of a 'Smarties' tube for tree trunk. Pack inside the base with Plasticine to weight it. Cover trunk with felt.

For tree top cut a 10 cm (4 in) diameter circle of fabric. Gather round edge, stuff, then turn raw edges to inside and place over top of trunk; pull up gathers to fit and fasten off. Remove trunk, spread round top edge with glue, press tree top in place.

Truck

Make and cover as for railway waggon. At front end glue on a felt-covered strip of card bent into an arch above truck. Add felt wheels and radiator.

Boat

Use a matchbox tray with one end cut off. Cut card base from pattern and glue under box, then stick a card strip all round boat. Reinforce boat then cover with felt and glue on braid.

Little people

Note: When using fabric strips for clothes, turn in raw edges and glue to neaten.

To make: Cut a 6 cm ($2\frac{3}{8}$ in) square of pink felt. Oversew two opposite edges together to make a tube, then turn right side out. Inside one end of tube slip a 2 cm ($\frac{3}{4}$ in) diameter card circle for base, and stick the felt edges just over edge of card. Weight the base with a lump of Plasticine, pushing it inside with a pencil, then stuff remainder. Gather and fasten off top edge, then tie a thread tightly round to shape neck, 2 cm ($\frac{3}{4}$ in) down from gathers.

Mark on eyes with pen or pencil. For man's hair cut a 2 cm ($\frac{3}{4}$ in) diameter circle of fur fabric or felt and sew it to top of head. For woman's hair sew centre of a few wool strands to forehead, then gather and sew strands to sides of head.

For man's cap cut a 2 cm ($\frac{3}{4}$ in) diameter circle of card, cover with fabric then bend slightly and stick to top of head. For bridegroom's top hat stick a small plastic lid covered with felt to top of cap.

Cover man's body by sticking round fabric strip, gathering at neck edge to fit neck. Make woman's dress top in same way, then gather and sew on a narrower strip of fabric for skirt. Glue on small pieces of fabric for headscarf, shawl, or lace for cap.

For railway guard's flag and fisherman's rod use cocktail sticks. Cut point off one end, glue other end firmly into figure. Glue on fabric flag or string for line.

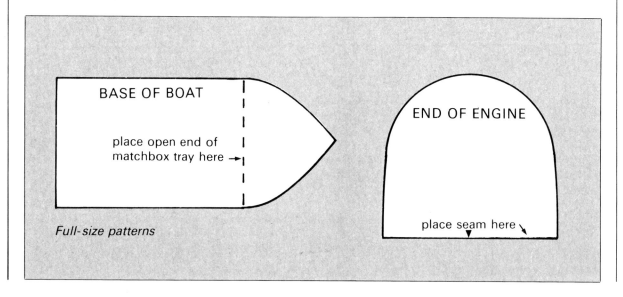

BASE OF BOAT

place open end of matchbox tray here →

END OF ENGINE

place seam here

Full-size patterns

Easter Bunny Puppet

This soft toy bunny, just 28 cm (11 in) high, also doubles as a hand puppet. The body is lightly stuffed, with an opening at the back allowing a hand to be put inside, so that the fingers and thumb can work the bunny's hands. There are also plenty of clothes for dressing up the toy.

You will need: Oddments of the following – fur fabric; thin cotton fabric for lining body and dress; printed fabrics; ribbon and trimmings for dress, bonnet, nightdress and pop-over pinafore; stuffing; brown and black felt and black embroidery thread for facial features; white fur fabric for tail; four small buttons and short lengths of elastic.

Notes: 5 mm ($\frac{1}{4}$ in) seams are allowed on all pieces unless otherwise stated.

The patterns are printed full-size on pages 136–8 for tracing directly off the page, but note that body front, base and dress front should be traced on to folded paper, placing fold to dot-and-dash line on pattern. After tracing, cut out and open up the folded pieces to give full-size patterns.

Cut out fur fabric pieces with smooth stroke of fur pile in the directions shown by arrows on the patterns. When cutting a *pair* of pieces, be sure to reverse the pattern when cutting the second piece.

The bunny

To make the body: Cut one body front from fur fabric and one from lining fabric. Mark arm darts on wrong side of fur fabric piece only, then stitch and trim darts. Tack lining and fur fabric pieces together round edges, wrong sides facing, except for lower edges.

Cut a pair of body back pieces from fur fabric and a pair from lining fabric. At centre back edge of one fur fabric piece, sew a loop of elastic to right side of fabric as shown on pattern (check that the loop will slip over your size of button). Now join centre back edges of each lining to centre back edge of

each fur fabric piece, with *right* sides of fabric together. Turn linings over to wrong sides of fur fabric pieces and tack raw edges together except for lower edges. Join centre back edges of body back pieces by oversewing them together on lining side, from A to neck edge, and from B to lower edge.

Now join body back to front at sides, round arms to neck edges, with fur fabrics together. Clip seams at corners. Lay body aside.

To make the head: From fur fabric cut a pair of head pieces and one head gusset. Join head pieces from point C through point E to neck edge. Now insert gusset round top and back of head, matching points C on gusset and head. Turn head right side out.

To assemble body and head: Slip neck edge of head right through neck edge of body (*see diagram 1, opposite*), with head inside body and matching points D and E. Backstitch head to body at neck seamlines. Turn right side out.

Stuff head firmly through the neck opening. Gather round raw neck edge of head (you can do this through centre back edges of body), then pull up gathers tightly and fasten off, to hold head stuffing in place.

Stuff all body pieces very lightly and evenly, inserting stuffing through lower edges between fur fabric pieces and linings. Tack linings to fur fabric at lower raw edges.

To insert the base: Cut one base piece from fur fabric and one from lining fabric. Tack them, wrong sides facing, around raw edges, pushing a little stuffing inside before completing tacking. Turn body wrong side out through back opening. Pin, then backstitch base to lower edge of body, fur fabric sides together and matching points F, G and H. Turn body right side out and sew button to back edge to correspond with elastic loop.

To make the tail: Cut, gather and stuff a 6 cm ($2\frac{1}{2}$ in) diameter circle of white fur fabric. Sew it to centre back of body, between points B and H.

To make the feet: Cut four foot pieces from fur fabric and join them in pairs round outer edges. Turn and stuff firmly, then oversew inner edges together. Sew inner edges to edge of base and body at front, spacing feet about 2 cm ($\frac{3}{4}$ in) apart.

To make the ears: Cut four fur fabric ear pieces and join them in pairs, leaving lower edges open; turn right side out and fold ears in half at lower edges, then oversew raw edges together as folded. Sew lower edges of ears to sides of head, about 2 cm ($\frac{3}{4}$ in) below head gusset, then sew again at gusset seamline.

To make the facial features: First trim fur pile slightly shorter all over face area. Cut nose from brown felt and pin it in place at the end of head gusset. Using double embroidery thread, work a stitch for mouth,

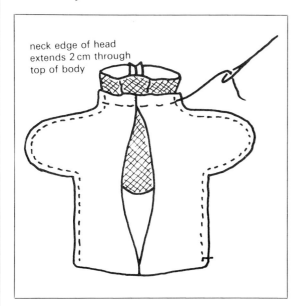

neck edge of head extends 2 cm through top of body

Diagram 1

2 cm ($\frac{3}{4}$ in) below nose, starting and fastening off thread underneath nose. Sew nose in place. Cut two eyes from black felt and work a highlight on each one in white thread. Sew eyes in place 3 cm ($1\frac{1}{4}$ in) apart, each side of nose.

The clothes

To make the dress: Cut dress front and one pair of backs from dress fabric. Sew elastic loop to right side of one dress back, where shown on pattern. Join front to backs at side edges, then sew on trimming above seam allowance at lower edge. Turn in seam allowance at all shoulder edges and press.

Cut and make dress lining in the same way, omitting elastic loop and trimming. Join lining to dress at centre back, armhole and neck. Clip curves in seams. Turn right side out and press. Slipstitch front shoulder edges of dress and lining to back shoulder edges.

For hem frill, cut a strip of dress fabric 5 by 60 cm (2 by 24 in). Make narrow hems on one long and both short edges. Gather the remaining long raw edge of frill to fit lower edge of dress and sew in place (leaving lining free), with right sides facing. Now turn in lower edge of lining and slipstitch it over seam. Sew button to back edge, opposite loop.

To make the nightdress: Add 4 cm ($1\frac{1}{2}$ in) to lower edge of dress front and back patterns, then make exactly as for dress. Sew trimming across yoke of nightdress and over armhole edges, then sew ribbon bow to front.

To make the pinafore: Use dress patterns but add 5 mm ($\frac{1}{4}$ in) to side edges, trim 5 mm ($\frac{1}{4}$ in) off lower edges of patterns and cut front neckline along dotted line shown on pattern. Make as for dress, but instead of frill at lower edge, sew on lace edging, easing it to fit round curve instead of gathering. Add ribbon bow.

To make the Easter bonnet: Draw and cut out paper patterns for bonnet and bonnet back to sizes shown in diagram 2 (*right*). Cut earhole out of bonnet pattern as shown.

Now cut one bonnet piece from fabric, placing pattern to fold in fabric as indicated. Cut out earholes and bind them with narrow bias strips of fabric. Cut bonnet back from fabric. Join back edge of bonnet to sides and curved top edge of bonnet back, clipping straight edge of bonnet to fit round curves in bonnet back. Neaten seam to prevent fraying. Make a narrow hem on lower edge of bonnet to form casing for elastic. Thread elastic through to gather lower edge slightly, then sew the elastic to each end of casing.

For bonnet frill cut a strip of fabric 7 by 40 cm (2¾ by 16 in). Fold it in half down length, right side inside; join short ends rounding off corners at folded edge. Turn right side out, gather and sew raw edges to face edge of bonnet. Bind raw edges with a bias strip. Add ribbons to tie under chin.

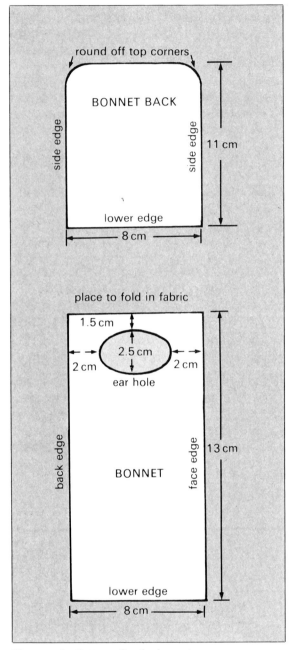

Diagram 2 Patterns for the bonnet

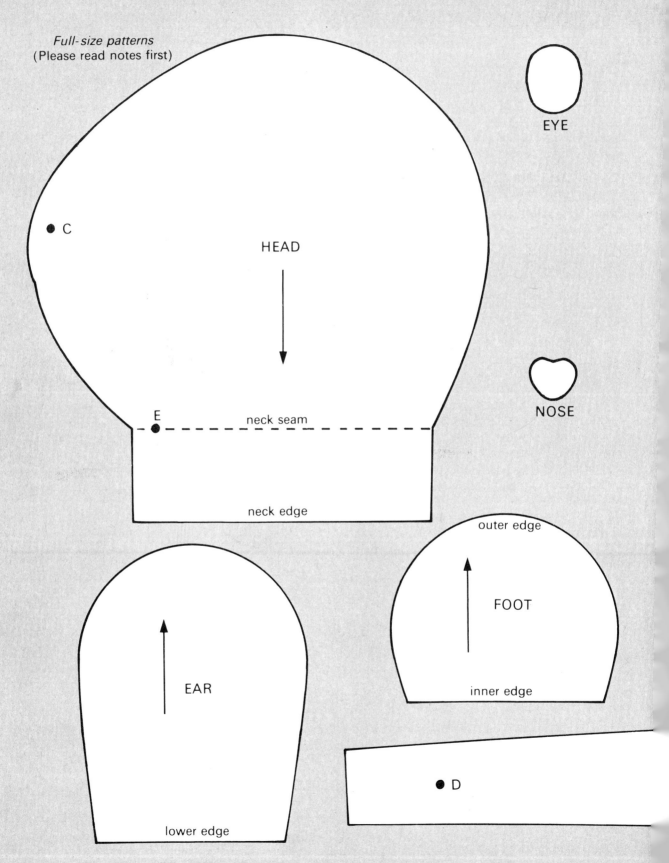

Full-size patterns
(Please read notes first)

EYE

● C

HEAD

↓

NOSE

E ●   neck seam

neck edge

outer edge

↑

FOOT

inner edge

EAR

↑

● D

lower edge

136

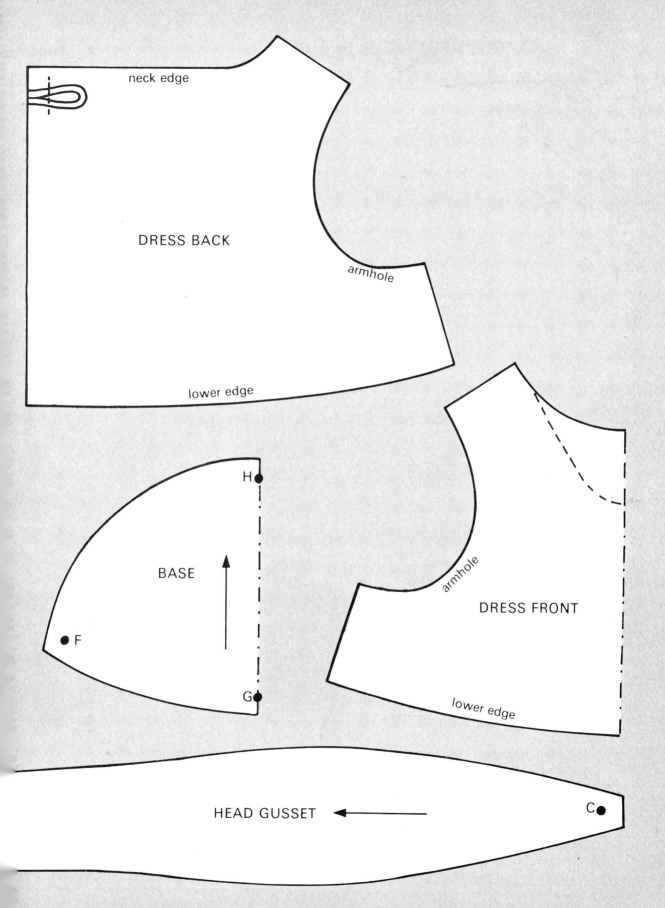

DRESS BACK

neck edge

armhole

lower edge

BASE

H

F

G

DRESS FRONT

armhole

lower edge

HEAD GUSSET

C

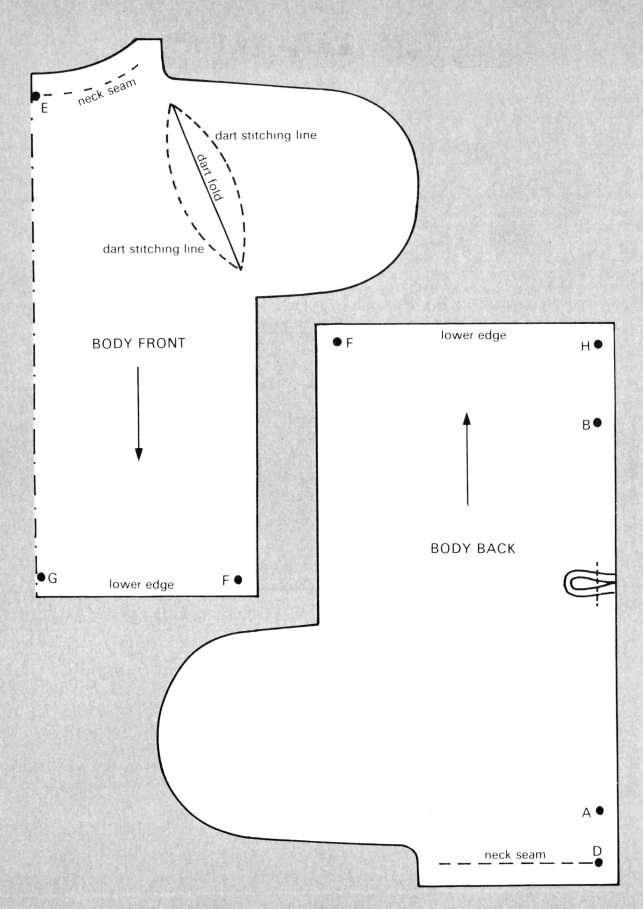

BODY FRONT

neck seam

dart stitching line

dart fold

dart stitching line

E

lower edge

G

F

BODY BACK

lower edge

F

H

B

A

neck seam

D

LIST OF SUPPLIERS

Beckfoot Mill,
Howden Road,
Silsden,
Nr Keighley,
West Yorkshire BD20 0HA
Tel. Steeton (0535) 53358
For fur fabric, felt, fillings, stockinette and all other toymaking accessories. Send 50p for complete catalogue (refunded on first order).

Griffin Fabrics Ltd,
The Craft Centre,
97 Claremont Street,
Aberdeen AB1 6QR
Tel. (0224) 580798
For fur fabric, felt, fillings, stockinette and all other toymaking accessories. Send 50p for complete catalogue (refunded on first order).

INDEX

Page numbers in italics refer to colour illustrations